Sui generis! A new genre of legal writing ... a gripping true story of one lawyer's obsession with seeking justice, revealing the human drama and its personal tolls. Dallas Plaintiff Attorney Kip Petroff's *Battling Goliath* is a modern-day parable of triumph over deceit and greed in the netherworld of America's mass tort litigation.

Petroff's saga meticulously details his decade-long quest for justice for the hundreds of thousands of injured victims of fen-phen, the inherently dangerous diet drug of the 1990s, manufactured and marketed by a huge and powerful pharmaceutical company. This unique first-person insight into the human tragedies spawned by the drug company provides a classic story of betrayal, downfall, and redemption.

With an engaging narrative in his debut expository storytelling, Petroff skillfully weaves the Byzantine maneuvering of his opposing legal titans confronting his passionate dedication for the victims whose hearts and lungs were irreparably damaged. His brutally honest style spares none, including himself, as he portrays the tragedies, grief, sorrow, and destroyed lives radiating from the wrongdoing of a pharmaceutical Goliath and its masters.

And ultimately, *Battling Goliath* is a cautionary tale for any society of the moral hazards of concentrated and unchecked power and wealth in the hands of a few. *Battling Goliath* is a must-read for patients, doctors, governmental regulators, lawyers, and anyone taking prescription medications.

R. Darryl Fisher, MD, JD
Cardiovascular Surgeon & Attorney, Oklahoma City

For people struggling to lose weight, the promise of a miracle pill is all too enticing. The pharmaceutical giant, Wyeth, took advantage of those desires in the name of profit, bringing the drug fen-phen to market with known deadly consequences to those taking it. This book is a compelling true life tale of the battle to bring justice to those without a voice and the immense toll it took on one man willing to take on Goliath.

Betty Murray, CN, HHC, RYT
Founder Living Well Health & Wellness
Author of *Cleanse: Detox Your Body, Mind and Spirit*

BATTLING GOLIATH

BATTLING GOLIATH
Inside a $22 Billion Legal Scandal

Kip Petroff with Suzi Zimmerman Petroff

Frame House Press, Inc.

Dallas, Texas

Frame House Press, Inc.
P.O. Box 12663, Dallas, TX 75225

First Edition

Book cover & design by goodmedia communications, llc
Authors' photographs by Robyn Hobbs Photography

The text in this book is set in Adobe Garamond Pro.

Manufactured in the United States of America
Printed by Taylor Specialty Books: Certified and Audited by the Sustainable Forestry Initiative (SFI) and Programme for the Endorsement of Forest Certification (PEFC).

Petroff, Kip.
    Battling Goliath : inside a $22 billion legal scandal
    / Kip Petroff ; with Suzi Zimmerman Petroff. -- 1st ed.
    p. cm.
    Includes index.
    LCCN 2011933898
    ISBN-13: 978-0-983-73740-7
    ISBN-10: 0-983-73740-1

    1. Products liability--Drugs--United States.
    2. Fenfluramine. 3. Phentermine.   I. Petroff, Suzi
    Zimmerman. II. Title.

KF1297.D7P48 2011   346.7303'8
                QBI11-600139

"... Whoever, whether an individual or group of individuals, was responsible for the whole fenfluramine situation, it's as reprehensible and criminal as the individuals who drove planes into the World Trade Center and bombed the Pentagon. I think that if we ever get a final accounting, we will find that these individuals were responsible for more deaths, more lasting damage. And the only way anything can be done to prevent this from happening again is by exposing it."

Dr. Leo Lutwak, Retired FDA Medical Officer
sworn deposition testimony

CONTENTS

THE TEN YEAR FEN-PHEN BATTLE

TIMELINE **1998** **1999** **2000** **2001** **2002**

**Pondimin & Redux
Removed from Market**
September 15, 1997

**Lovett
Trial & Verdict**
August 1999

**Trial Court Approval
of the Original Class
Action Settlement**
August 2000

**Echo
Disqual
Hearing
Aug/Sep**

**Plaintiffs' Management
Committee Appointed**
March 1998

**Screening
Period Begins**
January 3, 2002

**$4.8 Billion
Settlement
Announced**
November 1999

THE TEN YEAR FEN-PHEN BATTLE

2003	2004	2005	2006	2007	2008

Opt-Out
Deadline
May 3, 2003

Attorneys'
Fee Hearing
November 2007

Final Trial Court Approval
of the 7th Amendment
January 2007

Preliminary Trial
Court Approval of the
Seventh Amendment
August 2004

Screening
riod Ends
ry 3, 2003

Fee Order & Final
Payment Order
April 2008

PREFACE

LTHOUGH THIS STORY at times reaches seemingly
fictional proportions, it is a work of nonfiction. It is based
on facts recorded in trials, hearing or deposition transcripts,
as well as articles from newspapers, book chapters, and other verifiable
historical facts. This is also based on my handwritten notes from
conversations and court hearings that date from the beginning of the
fen-phen case in 1997 until I started using a computer in 2003, at
which point I began documenting everything in emails. My detailed
and dated notes served as a valuable resource to verify and confirm the
events and conversations recorded in these pages.

This litigation spanned more than a decade and has affected the
lives of over six million people. Because of the massive amount of
information in my files and at my disposal, one of the most difficult
tasks in writing this book was deciding what to include and what to
omit. I apologize to anyone who may feel as though the book fails to
adequately cover major events or players. This is my honest and best
attempt at concentrating millions of pages of fen-phen facts into this
present volume.

I wrote this book in first person because, as with every real
story, there are many different perspectives, each one as true to the
one experiencing it as it may be untrue to another. The only vantage
point for which I can be completely responsible is my own. I take full
responsibility for the manner in which these events are portrayed here.
I was present for all of it, and this is my true perspective.

INTRODUCTION

I N A COUNTRY preoccupied with food and plagued by obesity, weight loss has become a national obsession. Fads fail and dieting has become synonymous with starvation. Those who cannot lose weight the old fashioned way, through diet and exercise, hope for an easier, faster way—a magic pill.

One such hope lay in the drug Pondimin (fenfluramine), which was introduced in 1973. While Pondimin provided some weight-loss benefit, the accompanying drowsiness made it unpopular. The Food and Drug Administration (FDA) only approved it for short-term use, and Pondimin was of little interest to the public for its first two decades on the market. With support from Pondimin's owner, A.H. Robins, Dr. Michael Weintraub studied the effects of combining Pondimin with phentermine, an older, speed-like drug, and users lost weight without the drowsiness.

American Home Products (AHP), which later changed its name to Wyeth, bought A. H. Robins in 1989, and began marketing Pondimin through its Wyeth-Ayerst Laboratories Division. Weintraub's unpublished study debuted in medical journals shortly afterwards. By then, scientist Dr. Dick Wurtman had developed a drug similar to Pondimin that was marketed in Europe as Isomeride (dexfenfluramine) by Les Laboratoires Servier, a French company. Through another corporate buyout, AHP procured the rights to Isomeride and began marketing it as Redux (also through its Wyeth-Ayerst Laboratories Division) in the United States in June of 1996, turning AHP's diet drug domain into a full-fledged empire.

BATTLING GOLIATH

The drug combination was known as fen-phen. FENfluramine (brand name Pondimin) or its cousin dexFENfluramine (branded as Redux) were the "fen," and when PHENtermine is added to either one of these, the combination is known as fen-phen.

Magazines began publishing word of the "magic pill," and fen-phen became a household name. But with the rise in popularity, users also began reporting symptoms of primary pulmonary hypertension (PPH) and valvular heart disease (VHD). Many of these cases were reported to the drug company, but only a few were accurately reported to the FDA.

The first of these conditions, primary pulmonary hypertension, is a rare lung disease that constricts the arteries in the lungs and causes increased pressure, like crimping a garden hose as the water is running. The lungs must work harder to get the blood through the narrower vessels. Without correction, the patient will eventually suffocate. Primary pulmonary hypertension was, during the age of fen-phen, considered a death sentence.

But the most prolific of the drugs' side effects was valvular heart disease or VHD. In a normal functioning heart, the flow of blood is strictly one-way. In a heart with valvular heart disease, some of the blood fails to get through the valve opening, creating a two-way flow. The backward flow is known as regurgitation or leakage.

In the mid-1990s, there was little known about VHD and its relationship to fen-phen. Many panicked when the drugs were eventually removed from pharmacy shelves, and the media frenzy added to the mounting misinformation. Even those with normal echocardiograms (the test used to study the heart's anatomy) were afraid they might be dying. Most were already overweight and felt sluggish, and once they realized fen-phen could hurt them, many assumed it already had.

Some may argue that the fen-phen topic is old news. After all, the drug was removed from the pharmacy shelves in 1997. But, as of the publishing of this book in 2011, drug companies continue to put consumers at risk every day. Meridia was a diet drug introduced and removed from the market after reports of adverse side effects, and Alli and Xenical are diet medicines that have recently raised concerns from the FDA.

And it is not limited to just diet drugs. Vioxx, Baycol, Rezulin, Avandia, Propulsid, Duract, and other drugs, once household names due to their seemingly miraculous benefits, became infamous for their dangerous side effects. Anyone who has ever taken medication, or has given it to a child, parent, or other loved one, should understand the politics and economics behind the pharmaceutical industry, the Food and Drug Administration, and the ensuing courtroom battles that frequently follow the drug's debut into the consumer marketplace.

In truth, Pondimin and Redux were only minimally effective. The weight loss was temporary without major accompanying lifestyle changes, but the potential side effects were permanent. And, as with almost all drug side effects, risks increased the longer the drugs were taken.

More than a decade after fen-phen's removal from the market, there is still little consensus about its lasting effects. Many of those with heart valve damage will never display symptoms. Quite a few of those with the disease will remain at their present level, never getting sicker, but almost none will improve without some medical intervention. Some will get worse with time. The sickest may eventually need to have one or more of their heart valves repaired or replaced, and some of those will die from surgical complications. Perhaps the scariest of these facts is that, according to the American Heart Association and the American College of Cardiology, one in four aortic valve disease patients who die or experience heart failure from this disease do so before ever showing any symptoms.

Yet, prior to the drugs' removal, very few people who took fen-phen knew any of the potential risks. They believed that their doctors, the drug company, and the FDA were all serving as careful watchdogs for their health.

How then, critics wondered, could the company's doctors and scientists unleash such a beast? Bobby Sandage had been a key figure at Interneuron, a small pharmaceutical company that held the rights to Redux and acted as AHP's marketing partner. When it looked as though Redux might not receive FDA approval, he summed it up best: "We will stop at nothing to get this drug approved. Non-approval would ruin us financially." The commitment to "stop at nothing" permeated the litigation that followed. So, it all boiled down to one thing: profit. And profit there was! Annual sales of Pondimin, which had hovered around $3.5 million in 1993, shot up to an astonishing $177 million in 1995. AHP hoped to eventually make a billion dollars a year selling these drugs.

In March of 1995, Les Laboratoires Servier, the French pharmaceutical company that owned the rights to Redux in Europe, published a study that showed that incidents of PPH were ten times higher in those who took the drugs than the non-exposed general population. AHP downplayed this report to the FDA and chose not to fully disclose the new information in their Pondimin package insert.

AHP had received numerous reports of heart valve abnormalities from doctors by the mid-nineties, but the public was not warned about that condition until after the FDA approved Redux. Then finally, on July 8, 1997, just a year after Redux received FDA approval, the Mayo Clinic held a televised press conference announcing reports of new cases of drug-related heart valve surgery. AHP succumbed to public pressure, and Pondimin and Redux were pulled from pharmacy shelves nationwide on September 15, 1997. Redux, the new and improved Pondimin, lasted barely a year on the market before it was removed due to unacceptable side effects.

INTRODUCTION

An estimated six million people in the United States took Pondimin or Redux alone or in combination with phentermine, and many took both, the drug combination known as fen-phen. Fen-phen was not a fad diet. It was a doctor-supervised, dispensed-by-prescription-only medical protocol to treat the "new disease" of obesity. The drug cocktail was covered favorably in articles in almost every women's magazine in America including *Reader's Digest, Vogue,* and *Cosmopolitan.* For trusting consumers who took the drugs, theirs was a medically sound choice. There were no warning labels or package inserts about heart health damage until it was too late for most. Due to AHP's inadequate warnings, consumers had every reason to believe they were doing something good for their heart health when they used fen-phen to lose weight.

After years of litigation, there is little debate about the fact that the drugs caused PPH in a small percentage of users. The more typical injury, and the one that has spurred the most debate, is VHD, or the leakage of blood from the aortic and/or mitral heart valves. Too little was known about this type of injury and its relationship to fen-phen to put patients' minds at ease. All they knew was that it was serious but not usually immediately life threatening.

The confidence that their hearts would continue to beat strongly from one day to the next was replaced with fear and uncertainty. The company they held responsible was refusing to answer their questions. Fear turned to anger toward the greedy, indifferent company that had put them at risk in what appeared to be some massive human experiment. When it became clear that no branch of the United States government would champion their cause, worried consumers across the country hired attorneys, like myself, to help them hold the powerful pharmaceutical giants responsible.

What followed would become an epic war. The battles were unlike anything in the history of class action lawsuits. And, as the enemy infiltrated and infected our camp, the casualties were numerous.

Ultimately, the war we finished bore little resemblance to the war we began.

Battling Goliath is the true story of what happened when the American civil justice system became the only branch of government available to control and regulate a pharmaceutical industry that had grown bigger and more powerful than our federal and state governments combined.

ONE

ALONE

I T WAS MEANT to be a weekend of celebration with family. My parents rented a beach house in Destin, Florida, and the family came from all points to celebrate Mom and Dad's fiftieth anniversary. My older brother Ron came with his wife of twenty years, Karen, and my younger brother Bob brought his bride, Mary-Anne. I came alone; I was twice married and soon to be twice divorced.

The beautiful mid-October weekend offered perfect beach weather for those of us who came to enjoy each other's company rather than swim. The air was crisp, fresh, and sweet, not thick and salty as in the warmer months. The house was a typical beach house—living areas downstairs, sleeping rooms upstairs, nautical knick-knacks in every corner.

Mom cleaned, even though it was spotless when we arrived. She had to stay busy. Every time someone tried to lend her a hand, she shooed him or her away, and before long, as was always the case, we let her have the kitchen to herself.

Dad was eager to hear about his grandchildren. He beamed as I told him about Leandra's upcoming dance performance. She would be a star in *The Nutcracker*, and she was busy cheering for her school's football team. She had started driving, and that, alone, made for fun storytelling.

Ten-year-old Linnea would be sharing the stage with her older, more confident sister. Little Linnea was shy and had no problem letting her sister take the spotlight. "Linnea is a thinker," I explained. "She's not chatty, but you can see the wheels spinning in her mind."

Rendon, my middle child and only boy, was playing both baseball and football. Dad could hardly contain his pride at his grandchildren's busy lives.

I wanted to ignore my phone, but my caseload was thick with problems. My co-counsel were all handling important matters and knew I had taken the weekend off, but they promised to keep me updated if anything important arose. I ducked away to check my voicemail.

"Kip. This is Wayne. I know it's your parents' anniversary and you're trying to take some time off, but it's really important that I talk with you right away. Please call me on any of the numbers you have. It's Friday around four in the afternoon my time. Please call. Thanks." I looked at my watch and realized I had just missed him.

Wayne Spivey was one of my most trusted co-counsel, my eyes and ears in Philadelphia, the center of my ongoing litigation and the hometown of the drug company I had been suing. He worked for a respected law firm that served as my local counsel. Because I lived in Dallas, dropping in for a brief, early morning meeting in Philly meant making a two-day trip; for Wayne, it meant stopping by on his way to the office. He was my presence at meetings in Philadelphia, a way to ensure my voice was heard when it was not required for me to actually be there.

It was unlike Wayne to call to chat, so I excused myself from the celebration and found a private balcony. "Are you sitting down?" Wayne asked in a very serious tone.

"Yes," I lied, standing anxiously on the balcony overlooking the vacant beach. Laughter erupted from somewhere below. "What is it?"

"Man, it is hard to be the one to have to tell you this. I have it from a very reliable source that Scheff has a draft of a Civil RICO complaint that is going to be filed against you ... probably against Scott, too—maybe as early as Monday or Tuesday of next week."

I knew about the Racketeer Influenced and Corrupt Organizations Act, also known as RICO, because my law school professor, Robert Blakey, was one of the co-authors of the original statute. RICO is a federal law in the United States aimed specifically at organized crime. Under it, a person who is a member of a group that has committed any two of about thirty crimes inside a ten-year period can be charged. Federal authorities have a great deal of power, including seizing assets and using that seizure to force the defendant's hand. Jail time is also a possibility.

Suddenly it made sense why attorneys from the U.S. Department of Justice and the Food and Drug Administration had been so interested in my deposition of retired FDA scientist Dr. Leo Lutwak a few weeks earlier. It had seemed strange that the U.S. Department of Justice's lawyers were present considering the doctor was no longer in the FDA's employ.

Wayne explained, "Supposedly, this involves a bunch of things you guys did or failed to do regarding the fen-phen Nationwide Settlement."

A hot flash of fear shot through my body. I could lose everything I had worked for in my career, even if all they did was indict me. If they found me guilty, I could go to jail and miss watching my children grow up. These could be serious charges.

I was afraid to speak, certain I would vomit the moment I opened my mouth. Finally I managed, "Anything else I should know about?"

But Wayne had nothing more to offer.

The details were unimportant. Whatever they were, I knew they were lies. What mattered was the threat. Defending a RICO charge would ruin me financially and create numerous new problems. The thought made my head spin.

I stood on the balcony in shock as the waves crashed hard against the beach, competing with the sound of my heart pounding in my chest. Hot tears streamed down my face, and the fingernails of both my hands burned with pain. Looking down, I saw that I had dug them into the wood railing, forcing tiny chunks of stiff wood into the tender skin. My knuckles were pale and pronounced.

I released the railing and glanced around me. I was still alone—thank God—but the realization also bothered me. *I am so alone.*

Utter desperation and loneliness wormed their way under my skin, through the layers of muscle, and into my bones. I had no one. My children were too young to handle the news; my second wife and I were divorcing, and her attorney made sure I could not speak with her; and my family was trying to enjoy the celebration. I could not dump this on them, not now.

I allowed myself to indulge in the fantasy of walking into the water and letting the waves carry me out to sea where none of this could touch me. But I had done nothing wrong. This drug company wounded hundreds of thousands of people, killing many. It profited on their fears, permanently altered their hearts, filled millions of people with uncertainty, hid the truth, and fattened its own pockets in the process. I had been trying to uncover the truth, seek justice for the injured, and pay my bills.

The battle to protect and save the lives of thousands of people had suddenly changed into a battle to save my own life. I felt a renewed rush of compassion for the women and men I had been fighting all these years to help. More often than I cared to admit, I had allowed myself to think of these wounded and terrified victims as just cases or files, distancing myself from their pain. I now understood the deep fear weighing down each of them. Yes, they suffered from damaged hearts, but they suffered equally, if not more, from the fear of what their families might lose. The possibility that my children could lose their father sent waves of terror rippling through my body. I realized I was no longer fighting for the victims of fen-phen; I was fighting alongside them.

As I turned from the balcony to rejoin my family I prayed, *Please help me get through this. This is so much bigger and more powerful than anything I ever imagined. I have tried to live a good life. Help me through this, and I promise to do even better.*

ROUND ONE

TWO

GREAT EXPECTATIONS

I HAVE ALWAYS had a fighting spirit. I won seven major fistfights in seventh grade, the year my elementary school and three others merged into one junior high. I was not an angry kid; fighting was simply something boys at my school did. It was the social vehicle for establishing rank.

A few years earlier, my uncle had given me a subscription to *Sports Illustrated*, formally introducing me to the world of sports. Muhammad Ali had been stripped of his heavyweight title after being convicted of draft evasion during the Vietnam War. The *Sports Illustrated* story of his comeback affected me deeply.

Ali was a big talker. He had a way of intimidating his opponents that made him appear superhuman. Even more importantly, Ali was true to his beliefs. He cooperated in the entire draft process up until the point where he disagreed. It was all a matter of values—right over wrong.

My neighbor's dad had been a professional boxer, and all of his kids knew the sport. After many lessons-turned-beatings, the boys convinced me I would never make it as a boxer. When I was fourteen years old, I took a year off from fighting to nurse a knee condition, and consequently tried my hand at writing—I wrote my first novel. When I was fully healed, I decided to try something new.

Wrestling came naturally to me. I was good and quickly became accustomed to winning. The sport helped me to grow up, but it fell short of curing me of my troublemaking ways. Just three days before the Ohio state-qualifying tournament my senior year, a friend and I decided to pick a fight with one of our school's star football players, Mike Bonanno. We dumped pudding on his head, starting a nasty feud. I was suspended for two days; one more day of suspension and I would have been ineligible for the biggest wrestling match of my life. Fortunately, luck and Principal Verlaney were on my side.

Principal Verlaney may have been forgiving, but Bonanno was not. I humiliated him, and he fully intended to have his revenge that summer. He launched his attack by landing three solid swings of a tire iron across my lower back. Onlookers managed to pull him off, but the damage had been done. After daily visits to the team doctor, I was well enough to win seventh place at Nationals the following week, but my back was never the same.

The University of Arizona wrestling team offered me a spot, and I attended with hopes of qualifying for the Olympics four years later. Although I had been a star on my high school team, I found myself among many who were far better than me in Tucson. In the extraordinary company of my college teammates, I was pretty ordinary. My dreams of wrestling greatness were crushed.

It would make a much more moving story if I had stuck with it, worked out with Rocky Balboa-esque commitment, and through blood, sweat, and tears found a way to persevere. But my story is a little different. I was a realist who loved to win and knew there were not enough workouts or fights that could place me at the same level as my

Tucson teammates. I gave up my dreams of Olympic gold, quit the team, and finished the semester.

If wrestling was not my future, I could coach. I enrolled at Kent State the following semester where my older brother Ron was a student. Ron introduced me to Dr. Bernard Tabbs, a young English professor who, like me, was not content with mediocrity. Dr. Tabbs was a black man teaching at a mostly white college campus just a decade after the assassination of Martin Luther King, Jr. From the beginning, we had a strong connection, more than a professor-and-student relationship. We were friends.

He was always honest with me. "There's nothing wrong with being a coach," he told me. "Teachers are a gift; it's why I became one. We get to change people's lives, just like your coaches did for you and my own teachers did for me, and as I hope I am able to do some day. But Kip, you're so much bigger than that. You have the ability to save lives, not just change them."

Dr. Tabbs recognized that coaching had only been my choice because being a star wrestler was out of my immediate reach, but he knew it was not my calling. Thanks to Dr. Tabbs, my limitations gave way to my hungry fighter's spirit. "That, Kip, is your calling," he would say.

After finishing my undergraduate studies, I applied—and was surprised to be accepted—to University of Notre Dame Law School in South Bend, Indiana. Just as I was finishing law school and studying for the bar, Dr. Tabbs died of a brain aneurysm. He never made it to forty.

After graduation, I went to work for the Dallas firm of Strasburger and Price. While there, I handled two cases against attorney Lonnie McGuire. McGuire soon recruited me to work for his firm. Four years later, I partnered with long-time Dallas lawyer Judson Francis and have had my own firm ever since.

BATTLING GOLIATH

Everything is big in Texas, and that includes breast implants. I quickly went from "garden variety personal injury attorney" to being a "breast man," a term that was reserved for lawyers who sued on behalf of women with silicone gel implants. But, as scientific evidence weakened and manufacturer bankruptcies chipped away at our earnings potential, I was forced to move on to the next big thing.

In my then fourteen years of law experience, I had learned that the best way to build a reputation was to be the type of attorney my clients would be proud to recommend to their friends. But, while word-of-mouth might have been healthy for my professional reputation, it fell short of paying the bills. I also learned the secret to using the media without appearing overly commercial. A short newspaper article about one of my breast implant cases had sent the phones ringing years earlier. I quickly learned just how closely people pay attention to the news.

"I'm headed home," Redonda said one autumn afternoon in 1997, removing her reading glasses and placing them on her desk for the next day. Redonda Gregg had been my secretary and loyal friend for eight years. "You need anything before I leave?" I heard nothing. Office work was a chore for me, and if Redonda was going to be able to read my notes, they had to be legible. It was hard enough for me without distractions.

"What on earth?" Redonda was standing behind me, her tiny manicured hand on my shoulder and her voice booming in my ear. Suddenly I realized the last sixty seconds of talking had been directed toward me.

"I'm making the news. Trying anyway. I'm going to file Nancy Lewis's case tomorrow and see if anyone's interested." She reached around me, corrected the heading, and circled two words I had misspelled. She would be typing it first thing in the morning and could have made the changes then, but she enjoyed proving to me that I should have just let her do it in the first place.

While she took charge, I checked my watch and reached for my hidden bottle of Grey Goose Vodka. There was enough for at least two drinks. I wondered if Redonda would be joining me or if I would get them both. *No worries,* I thought. *I have plenty more at home.* By the time I turned back to my desk, Redonda had produced only one clean glass—I would be drinking alone. It was after five, so I was allowed.

"My new client has agreed to go public. So I'm trying to see if Channel 8 will bite." I kicked back in my seat, pleased with my day's accomplishments but ready to unwind. "Maybe some of the others, too ... Channel 4, maybe 5 or 11."

Redonda hit the switch on the copier, and the quiet room got even quieter.

"I'll be in early so you can make changes to that thing." She pointed to the draft of the "Plaintiff's Original Petition," Texan for "You're gettin' sued."

Redonda left, but I still had plenty of work to do. My twelve-year marriage had just ended a few months earlier, and my three children lived with their mother. Without them around, my house seemed huge and lonely. Other than being with my children and practicing law, I did not have much of a life. Dating was something I had dabbled in on the side when work failed to keep me busy enough. Besides, there were loose ends to be tied up on my remaining breast implants cases. And then there was this new diet drug case, too.

One last look at the petition ensured it had all the words the news reporters liked to quote: "gross negligence," "punitive damages," "pain and suffering," "mental anguish," and the like. *This is going to be big,* I thought.

The popular diet drug fen-phen had been removed from the market two weeks earlier, and it surprised me that no one had filed a lawsuit yet. Mine would be the first in Dallas County, and if this was as big as I anticipated, being first was newsworthy. It meant there were a lot of former fen-phen users who had not yet learned the dangers surrounding the drugs they had taken. My news story would encourage them to get help right away, and if they discovered their hearts were damaged, hopefully they would also come to me to seek justice.

We filed the lawsuit the next morning. Redonda faxed copies of the petition to the major news outlets. The ticking of my office clock seemed to grow louder as the minutes turned to hours. The silence of the office phone only made the tick, tick, tick increasingly unbearable.

"Maybe the lines are down."

"Checked them. Everything's working great."

"Did the fax go through?"

"Got a confirmation page for every news station."

Maybe the story isn't as big as I thought. But Pondimin and Redux had been wildly successful and had just been found to be wildly dangerous. *This is newsworthy*, I hoped.

I tried to occupy myself with busy work, but the quiet of the phone was too distracting. Finally, I heard the familiar buzz, and line one blinked. I held my breath and heard Redonda's familiar voice. "Kip, it's Kathi on line one." My ex-wife was the last person I wanted clogging the lines when I was expecting calls from the media. I kept it brief and quickly got back to more important things—waiting.

The first real call was from the *Dallas Morning News*. Shortly thereafter we heard from two of the television stations. All three media outlets would be turning our little petition into big news.

Redonda was at the office before me the next morning. Her hair, normally Aqua Net perfect, was pushed carelessly to the side. It was obvious she had already been busy, and at not quite eight o'clock in the morning, that was good news for me. She told me she had arrived to find the office answering machine maxed out. "There's no telling how many calls we missed because there was no tape left in the recorder!" I stuck a McDonald's coffee in her hand, and the two of us got straight to work.

The stories on TV the night before and in the morning paper had generated huge interest, and I was the only lawyer mentioned. That the answering machine had failed to record a few messages did not bother me. *They will call again*, I hoped. And they did.

THREE

GETTING INSIDE THE GIANT'S HEAD

ONLY WEEKS BEFORE I had worried that my little story was too little. It soon became apparent that the opposite was true. The number of people contacting me about potential lawsuits had started to feel overwhelming. My already too-small office would need to accommodate an additional attorney, sooner rather than later. Just about the time Redonda and I had cleared away enough room, the perfect man for the job became available.

I knew Robert Kisselburgh from when he had worked as a summer law clerk at McGuire and Levy early in my career. He was from California but had no trouble blending in with the Texas good ol' boys. When he wore his cowboy boots, you got the sense that he meant it. He had even picked up the habit of chewing tobacco. My Midwestern feet, on the other hand, never took to cowboy boots, not even the expensive custom pair my former boss and close friend Lonnie McGuire had given me. And I preferred cigars to chewing tobacco, vodka over cold beer. I was not a native Texan and was certainly not a good transplant, like Robert.

Ten years after Robert first walked into McGuire and Levy, and just as fen-phen was becoming scandalous, his boss, and my former boss, Lonnie McGuire, announced his retirement. The firm would be closing, Robert needed a job, and his quick understanding of the complex fen-phen situation made him the ideal choice.

One of Robert's first tasks was helping to get the new lawsuits filed in court. A distinct advantage to being the first party to file is that the plaintiff chooses when and where to do it. But merely filing the cases is not enough; they have to be filed correctly or defendants could try to move them to another less convenient or sympathetic court. Savvy defense lawyers are experts at moving lawsuits—like chess pieces—in ways that give them a distinct advantage.

Keeping cases in state court and close to home is always ideal, especially in Texas. For me, speed has always been the name of the game, and with personal injury cases, state courts are almost always preferable to federal courts, where judges can be unsympathetic to the plaintiffs' cause. And Texas judges are known for preferring to wrap up cases more quickly than most.

On the other hand, if our cases did get stuck in federal court, they would be forced into the Multi-District Litigation (MDL), the massive umbrella for cases like ours at the federal court level that attempts to streamline the legal process. An MDL does this by organizing discovery requests and other tedious legal matters once rather than the hundreds or thousands of times it would have to be done if each case were tried individually. This allows one federal judge to handle the details in one court, freeing dozens of judges nationwide from worrying about them until the preliminary issues are resolved.

To simplify and cluster the various scattered cases piling up in the federal system, the Judicial Panel on Multi-District Litigation (the JPMDL) formed the fen-phen MDL three months after Pondimin and Redux were withdrawn from the market. We were particularly concerned with the infamously slow pace of most MDL proceedings.

Understanding all of this, and using it to his advantage, is what made Robert the best man for the job. Almost immediately, he discovered that two phentermine manufacturers, Medeva Pharmaceuticals and Zenith Goldline, had offices in Tarrant County, Texas. The local connections, along with a creative conspiracy theory, gave us the power to file and keep the suits in our own backyard.

The more we worked together, the more we perfected our rhythm and pace. Before long, we were functioning like two halves of the same brain, and we were fast. AHP, on the other hand, was a slow-moving behemoth—unquestionably big and tremendously powerful but lacking the agility to move with speed. Nowhere was this more apparent and potentially damning than when it came to our discovery requests.

American Home Products received our written interrogatories and a request for production of documents in October of 1997. This was my chance to shake things up a bit, agitate the giant, and see what information would funnel down through the system before anyone had the chance to censor it. When asked for the equivalent of a file cabinet, they produced what amounted to a post-it note, forcing me to counter with even more determination. If we were going to have a chance, we needed every fen-phen-related document from every AHP employee from day one to the present. It was the traditional defendant-plaintiff tango: AHP would pull away from us, and we would pull back even harder.

One of their attorneys called asking for more time, which we expected. We offered them another ninety days if they would allow us to come to their offices in Philadelphia to inspect their New Drug Application (NDA) file, which was already a matter of public record at the FDA. They agreed.

Robert was less than pleased with my victory. "The NDA will help us establish a chain of command so we can get an idea of who does what at the drug company, what AHP people looked like, how they talk and what they're thinking," I explained. "Who do we request depositions from? We need to develop a timeline and a list of documents to ask for as well as questions to ask so we can start putting facts together, and so we can make better discovery requests. Basically, we need to find out how to become bigger pains-in-the-ass to this company," I argued.

Robert got it. Having him on my side was reassuring. He was the type of attorney who, despite being the new guy, forced me to provide logical reasons for my fiery passions. He was conservative and I was a risk-taker. Together, we were becoming the powerhouse our clients needed to defeat AHP.

The sound of snowplows outside my window woke me before my six fifteen morning wake-up call. It was something I had missed in my dozen or so years living in Texas. The sound reminded me of my childhood days in Ohio. The snow, along with the excitement of the day's treasure hunt, made it easy for me to feel fully awake before I had even had my coffee.

Robert's southern California roots and easy Texas adaptation positioned him for a vastly different opinion about snowy St. Davids, Philadelphia. At breakfast, he mumbled something about his room being cold and the waiter being late with his coffee. It was going to be a long day. Stress was a built-in feature to the task ahead, so survival depended on not allowing his mood to dampen my own. After all, it felt like home to me.

GETTING INSIDE THE GIANT'S HEAD

We had both been to the corporate headquarters of big companies we had sued before, but this was something very different. There were several receptionists at the front desk busily answering calls with a large, lighted map of the world looming impressively behind them. Tiny lights represented various cities around the world, each boasting a place where the Wyeth Ayerst Laboratories Division of American Home Products had offices.

"Goliath Wyeth," I mumbled. The whole place made me feel small, just as David must have felt as he stood before the incredible ogre, tiny slingshot in hand.

A representative from the law department appeared and led us to a revolving door. She instructed us with flight attendant enthusiasm: "Walk halfway through and then stop when the door stops moving." We gave each other comical looks—part *Farewell, it was nice knowing you* and part *Can you believe this?*

Robert went first. Technology was one of his passions, and he appeared to be absorbing every detail. He walked halfway through and stopped. The door behind him closed, and the door in front of him remained shut. He was momentarily trapped between the door going in and the door going out. The metal detector scanned him, and then a short burst of air shot upwards between his cowboy boots. Only his backside was visible to me, but I knew he was grinning ear to ear. Robert, normally militarily perfect in his appearance, passed the test, but his hair did not. Once at the other side, he pressed it back into place and turned to watch me.

Like Robert, my scan was clean. I joined him on the other side and chuckled, "Feels like *Star Trek*." The lawyer escorting us shot us both looks of disapproval.

We knew we were coming to view a file and had two days to do it. Nothing could have prepared us for what awaited. Our escort took us to a small, windowless room filled with numerous bankers boxes, each filled with documents. She then introduced us to two law clerks.

Their jobs were to sit in the room with us. "So you can tell them if you need anything," she explained before warning us that we were not permitted to leave the room alone for any reason.

The clerks huddled in a corner with the law books they were reading as if they had been told to be as invisible as possible. Robert began checking out the room where we would work for the next two days. "Smile for the camera," he said as he looked around the room for signs of one.

It was almost ten o'clock before we finally got to work. The file was comprised of nineteen boxes, each stuffed with about two thousand pages of information detailing the Pondimin New Drug Application. It contained every piece of paper related to obtaining and sustaining FDA approval to market fenfluramine (under the brand name Pondimin) in the United States and periodic reports sent to the FDA after approval. There were references to tests and analyses performed on the fenfluramine molecule back in the sixties and also more recent testing documentation.

The plan was for me to start at box one and move up in order. Robert would start at box nineteen and work down. He seemed to have gotten the better end of the deal. My box, which represented the oldest material, was the initial research on the sex lives of rats as it related to the drugs. Robert had more recent items.

After a short while, he got my attention with a document that listed every attorney who had ever sent a written complaint to AHP in relationship to the drugs. It was too good to be true. Neither of us had expected a "how to sue AHP" roadmap, so we teamed up, ignoring the other eighteen boxes, and copied down every detail of Robert's find.

The rest of the two-day period was spent carefully and meticulously picking through each document. As expected, we did not find anything that would crack the case, but Robert's impressive list of questions was the rough outline of an attack plan. Is phentermine responsible? What role did the phentermine companies play in all this? What was the FDA told and what did they do about it? Did the FDA know about all the facts we had just learned in our two days at the home office? What did the doctors know when they prescribed these drugs in combination for longer than is recommended in the package inserts?

We had the foundation for a strategy, a list of documents we wanted to request, witnesses we wanted to depose, and an unexpected roll call of attorneys who had a beef with AHP. Plus, we had enough information to begin conducting the first fen-phen seminars for plaintiffs' lawyers in the country, funneling dozens of attorneys and thousands of cases our way.

FOUR

PREPARING FOR BATTLE

THE TARRANT COUNTY Steering Committee was formed in early 1998 to act as the plaintiffs' liaison between the defendants and the Tarrant County District Courts. As we expected, Mike McGartland would prove the best choice to lead the charge in North Texas. He was a natural networker; he could make each person in a crowd feel like they were the most important one there.

Even more impressive was his ability to get things done. At the very moment he was being named chairman, he proved he deserved it. Like a coach rallying his team, he informed us that his goal would be to develop the cases quickly and make document and deposition requests early and often. "And then we'll request trial settings as soon as we have a full docket with willing lawyers—strike while the iron's hot!"

The formation of the Tarrant County Steering Committee gave the plaintiffs a united voice and established Fort Worth as the statewide epicenter of fen-phen litigation. McGartland developed streamlined discovery procedures that funneled otherwise scattered evidence directly to him. He constantly demanded that American

Home Products produce better information, witness depositions, and documents, keeping the drug company and its expensive defense team on their toes.

In the meantime, *The Texas Lawyer* featured my firm in their front page story: "FAT CITY: *The Fen-phen Feeding Frenzy*," with the subtitle, "The scramble's on in what could be the mother of all mass-tort litigation." I had never thought of myself as a mass tort lawyer, someone who makes a living focusing on masses of similar cases. Mass tort lawyers hope to cash in on the sheer volume of cases, taking a percentage of each recovery. Even with one hundred breast implant clients, I knew each and every one, and it seemed small, not massive. But this was different. It was the first time my cases were featured on the front page of a popular legal magazine. This felt massive.

The article presented me in the light I had hoped: a confident attorney seeking fair compensation for his clients from the powerful corporation that injured them. It also presented the fen-phen fiasco as disjointed, complex, and costly. It was word-of-mouth advertising from a trusted source, and I had no doubt it would bring in more referrals.

For a split second, I found myself fantasizing about getting rich off this case. I held the magazine in my hands, glanced down at my name and smiled. *Keep your eye on the goal, Kip*, I reminded myself. *This is about changing people's lives, even saving them, not money or fame.* I had to keep my head on straight.

I tossed the article into the desk drawer. Depositions were right around the corner, and I needed to prepare for battle. I could not allow anything to distract me.

🏛

Another part of my strategy was to get into the courtroom as soon as possible, and in order to do this I needed to start getting information from AHP insiders through a series of legal interviews or depositions. I made immediate arrangements to depose the AHP director of medical affairs, Dr. Marc Deitch. He had signed the letter to doctors announcing the removal of the drugs from the market.

The defense balked at the aggressive timing of the depositions. It is customary to wait until all of the documents for the case are gathered and both sides have had a chance to analyze them. But waiting was not my style; more time would give the defense a chance to coach the good doctor. We were working closely with McGartland's Fort Worth team, so we devised a plan for us to attack early and share information with them, and they would attack later—after the document production—and share information with us.

I struck a deal with the defense to take Deitch's deposition right away by promising it would be my only one. By acting early and asking the right questions, I could get the drug company committing early to facts and positions it might later regret.

🏛

I was already on my second drink when Robert entered the near-empty Philadelphia hotel bar. "This is a trial lawyer's finest hour," I toasted, empty glass in hand, promptly ordering a fresh replacement.

Robert ordered a bourbon and Coke and took a seat, leaving a stool between us. He waited for his drink to arrive and sat staring into the rows of bottles on the opposite side of the bar. Our drinks came, so I finished our toast, adding, "We're finally going to start getting some answers."

"Yep." He took a small sip and continued studying the bottles. A stranger might think he was being rude, but I knew this was Robert's thinking mode, how he prepared for battle. Knowing that it was best not to push him to talk when he was like this, I pressed on anyway.

"Thank God there isn't a rule that says you can't ask questions if you don't know the answers," I continued sarcastically, "Because I plan to spend the next two days doing exactly that."

Pins and needles pricked at both my knees, and my lower back was on fire, both reminders of my reckless teen years and all the fighting. I would be going into battle the next day, and before it had even begun, I hurt. As we sat there in silence, I wondered if we had gotten ourselves into the ass kicking of a lifetime. I guess if we had, I was glad Robert was on my side.

I threw back the last few drops of liquid courage and pain reliever. "We're going to have some fun tomorrow," I said to Robert. He flicked his finger at the wadded cocktail napkin in front of him. It sailed across the bar and into the trashcan ten feet away, a very unlikely shot.

"Yep."

I was awake by five thirty the next morning, and by six forty-five I was already prepping the room for the nine o'clock deposition. Notebooks reserved our seats. Within moments, the videographer wheeled in his equipment and found the perfect vantage point.

After a quick breakfast, Robert and I returned together just moments before we were scheduled to begin. Men and women in dark suits balanced cups of hot coffee and folded *USA TODAY*s. They milled about in the hall, near the doorway and in the room. We had reserved a room big enough to seat fifty, and it was packed.

We carefully navigated our way through the maze of precariously perched cups, enjoying the statement our casual appearance made. We carried large (but half-empty) briefcases, and in a lawsuit in which no paperwork had been exchanged, this signaled we possibly had something they lacked.

Somewhat ironically, many of the lawyers did not know who Robert and I were. Our slacks, knit shirts, and Robert's cowboy boots stood in sharp contrast to the sea of starched shirts, silk ties and shiny shoes. All doubts about our identity were removed when we took two of the four vacant seats we had reserved at the front of the very long table. I adjusted my microphone, and my long-awaited chance to take the first fen-phen deposition became reality at exactly nine o'clock.

The court reporter already had many of the attorneys' business cards lined up in order, and I used these to put names and faces together. Most of those present appeared to be at least a decade older than the two of us. Senior attorneys were generally reserved for important cases, which validated my theory that this was such a case.

The defense identified themselves and their clients before we began the deposition. The only plaintiffs' lawyer there besides Robert and me was Bill Clark, an attorney from Tyler, Texas. He had jumped on the fen-phen bandwagon early as well.

One other person stood out among all the others that morning. It was difficult to miss the tall, white-haired man sitting near the front of the table next to Bill. I assumed at that point that he was a defense attorney like all of the others. He was very tall, at least six foot three with a fatherly and compassionate face. "I'm Gary Huber. I represent the truth," he said to the court reporter as roll call continued.

Dr. Huber was not an attorney, but instead a well-known Harvard-trained physician who had notoriously battled the tobacco industry. The doctor had attended the deposition with Bill Clark. Like AHP, he was being sued, but because he had written many fen-phen prescriptions. When he discovered AHP failed to disclose the drugs' dangers, he was furious, and not because he was named in the suit. Instead, he was upset that he had unknowingly put people he cared about at risk. He had taken on the tobacco industry twenty-five years earlier in search of the truth; now he was prepared to join the lawyers who were suing him because he felt like he owed it to his patients.

As I approached the microphone, anyone who was still standing quickly grabbed a chair. It was serious business, and I enjoyed commanding the attention of nearly a thousand combined years of legal experience with such ease.

With the exception of the rhythmic scratching of ink pen on pale yellow paper, the room full of chattering suits was silent by the time AHP's Medical Affairs Director, Dr. Mark Deitch, answered the third question: why had the drugs been abruptly removed six months earlier? His facial expressions gave way to intense furrows of concentration.

"We had learned of information suggesting that in patients without any symptoms, there was evidence of changes on echocardiograms."

When asked to explain, he squirmed uncomfortably but eventually admitted that there was evidence of heart valve damage in relationship to fen-phen. And he tried to say that the decision to pull the drugs had been made as soon as the company learned of the trend.

Past experience had proven that Deitch had a habit of dodging questions by saying, "That depends on how you define it." He quickly shed that habit when I repeatedly referred to the dictionary I had brought to the deposition. Soon, he was telling me everything I wanted to know—each of his words a brushstroke on an otherwise blank canvas.

At the end of the first morning, I looked through my thin notebook of topics checking off those that had already been covered. Almost everything. We had almost accomplished in one morning what I had hoped would be two days' work. Finishing early would be an admission that we were thin on evidence.

During a working lunch break in my room, a cold cup of weak hotel coffee I had brought up from the bar sat untouched. I propped the door open so Robert could let himself in and returned to my notes. Robert poked his head in. "You did a fine and workmanlike job back there, Tiger." He was in a much cheerier mood than I.

"Yep," I replied jokingly.

"How are you going to stretch this out another day and a half?" It was the same question I had already been asking myself.

Before I could answer, Bill Clark, the attorney who had accompanied Dr. Huber to the deposition earlier in the day, stuck his head in the open door. "Mind if I come in for a minute? I've got something you might want to see." Bill, normally outwardly friendly, was instead very serious. "You got balls going after this guy before you have the company documents," he started. "You're doing the right thing. I wouldn't have the guts to do it on a big stage like this, but maybe what I'm going to show you will help."

He handed me two letters on AHP letterhead. "I'm not allowed to tell you who gave these to me. They're letters that the drug company sent to doctors a while back. One of those doctors gave them to someone who gave them to me."

The names of the doctors had been blacked out, but the city, Houston, was still visible. The letters explained that, while AHP was not outwardly pushing the fen-phen combination, they did urge doctors to check out studies from someone named Weintraub who had encouraging things to say about the combo.

I thanked Bill and pledged anonymity to him and his secret source. "After all," I laughed, "Why would I tell anyone you gave them to me when I can look smart for getting them on my own?" He flashed his friendly smile and disappeared into the hallway. Robert took one letter and I started on the other.

"We must be living right, Cowboy," I said to Robert clutching the pot of gold in my hands.

"Yep."

AHP's lawyers were stunned that afternoon when we provided them copies of their client's own correspondence. And while our evidence failed to rattle Deitch, his attorneys' behavior did. He was more than willing to express his frustration, shooting the defense team scornful glances for validating the importance of our find.

The letters provided enough questions to make full use of our first and second day. Deitch and his teams of lawyers didn't have time to think up canned answers or wiggle their way around the facts. He was forced to tell the truth.

We made arrangements to store the documents from our many discovery requests in the basement of McGartland's Fort Worth office building. The full scope of the situation became almost comical when we learned it would be two semi trucks full of boxes.

The documents were delivered within three days, exactly as promised. Two weeks later, Robert had a dozen law clerks from Southern Methodist University and Texas Wesleyan Law School carefully sifting through and cataloging each item.

Over the next few weeks, we were scheduled to depose fifteen witnesses, a "Who's Who" of fen-phen. Our battle plan was coming together: a unified attack against AHP across a swath of North Texas covering over almost two hundred miles—from Van Zandt County in the east, across Dallas, Tarrant, Johnson and Nolan Counties to the west.

Robert's main responsibility was organizing and then understanding the evidence. He and a team of law clerks culled through the hundreds of thousands of documents, identifying what was of value and keeping an ongoing list of gaps.

McGartland would use Robert's ongoing list to convince the drug company to provide additional material to fill the gaps. For example, a simple reference to a meeting would prompt McGartland to demand files from every person at the meeting. He became an irritation to American Home Products, but every request produced something we might not have gotten otherwise. As the leader of the Tarrant County Steering Committee, he had almost immediate access to Fort Worth judges when needed, and this constant judicial threat prompted a more cooperative attitude from the defense.

Mike Schmidt practiced law just a few blocks from my office. He had handled cases for injured plaintiffs, but he had also defended the companies, so he was experienced on both sides of a lawsuit. When we put the word out that we were looking for help with our documents, Schmidt was the first to step up.

Schmidt also acted as liaison between our camp and a powerhouse team of great Houston lawyers who were also gathering cases. Plus, he was about twenty years older than the rest of us thirty-somethings, and in the youthful company we were keeping, age equaled credibility.

My job was to take the lead in questioning the witnesses. I used the Deitch deposition as an outline and then used Robert's selected documents to build from there.

The fifteen depositions scheduled later that summer became my main focus, and Robert spent most of his time preparing for them by refining our information. McGartland continued his public bickering with AHP's lawyers and finally pushed them over the edge.

"We've really got them on the ropes now, boys," McGartland boasted as Robert and I listened on speakerphone one afternoon. AHP's attorneys had filed an Emergency Motion for Temporary Relief and a Petition for Writ of Mandamus based on what they called "impossible discovery orders" that McGartland had secured from a cooperative Tarrant County judge. If granted, both would have slowed us to a rate akin to the snail-paced MDL. Unfortunately for AHP, both were denied by the Court of Appeals.

They then took their Mandamus Petition to the Supreme Court

of Texas, had it denied the same day, and then revised their Emergency Motion and immediately re-filed it in the same court.

McGartland's voice crackled with enthusiasm. "And that's just the update from the last week!"

The Supreme Court of Texas never ruled on the discovery disputes. McGartland shed light on the corporation's stalling tactics and AHP withdrew the Emergency Motion. They opted instead to file a request for statewide consolidation of all fen-phen cases, something similar to an MDL at the state level. This would have been suitable for the sluggish pace with which corporations are accustomed, and it could have put the brakes on our momentum.

Judge Fred Davis would be in charge of all fen-phen cases in Tarrant County courts. Much to our relief, he announced that there would not be a single judge to oversee fen-phen cases for the entire state, as had been rumored.

Judge Davis was a reasonable man, well liked and trusted. Robert was especially impressed. "Nothing keeps defense lawyers in line like having weekly status conferences with a judge like Davis," he gloated on a conference call one afternoon. For those less familiar with him, he went on to explain that this particular judge would not give the defense any reason to object or appeal. "He'll set trial dates far enough out to keep the defense happy and close enough to satisfy Kip."

A few weeks later, his predictions proved spot-on when Davis entered an order requiring AHP to produce missing documents and privilege logs. No one objected.

AHP had naturally been reluctant to give up internal company documents, especially when doing so could cost it millions or even billions of dollars in damages. We understood this, but our job was to accomplish exactly what AHP was trying to prevent. Our team's approach kept constant pressure on its lawyers, forcing them to respond daily to our demands, and as a result, the damaging evidence continued to flow our direction.

PREPARING FOR BATTLE

On June 1, the Tarrant County Document Depository received several hundred thousand additional items long before anyone else in the country—and just in time. Our first Dallas deposition was scheduled to begin in less than two weeks, and Robert and his law clerks, now experienced document analysts, were opening the boxes before they were off the truck.

🏛

It was around this time that I met Leslie Geer, a fen-phen defense attorney representing some doctors who had been named in suits. I had been divorced about two years, and it seemed like the right time to start dating. Once I finally mustered the courage to ask her out, we were a couple. She was just what I needed in my life: simple, kind, and not at all demanding.

Because I took my work, my children, and my drinking very seriously, I made a point never to mix them. From the time I got up each morning until at least five in the afternoon, I was either an attorney or a father, neither of which was improved by vodka. Once I picked up my first glass, which was always after five o'clock, I was a dedicated drinker. Leslie understood. No woman in my life had ever given me that sort of space and freedom.

🏛

Robert and I spent our summer both preparing for and taking AHP depositions. There were many of them, and all proved consuming. Because we were allotted only one day to complete each, we insisted on starting precisely at nine o'clock each morning, and AHP's lawyers would pull the plug at exactly five each evening.

The AHP side of the depositions, however organized, was much less predictable. Each was a new experience as witness after witness brought a unique style of answering, or in some cases, evading

35

questions. Some of the witnesses seemed to have very poor memories of recent events, and others clearly were not interested in cooperating, but we had documents we could now use to help them recall and to encourage cooperation and truthfulness.

We plaintiffs had the same two lawyers asking all the questions, but AHP rotated its lineup of lawyers, each of whom had a different style, creating a variety of unique climates. We were starting to see how this played into their game plan, and we entertained ourselves by trying to predict who would be pulled from the bench for upcoming witnesses.

Robert's document analysis team was diligent even in the midst of ongoing depositions. They continuously faxed or couriered new findings from the Fort Worth Depository to our office. There, Redonda or one of her crew would organize and copy them and then deliver them across town to me. It was typical of Robert to present me with important evidence moments before he expected me to use it, often while I was questioning a witness. He usually knew better than I how the document fit with that witness's testimony, so he would quickly brief me with a hand-written sticky note. But I was still at an advantage over AHP's defense. They rarely had a clue as to the exhibit's existence until the moment it was labeled and introduced with the camera rolling and court reporter typing.

This organized chaos became part of our strategy. Each member of our small team seemed to possess a sixth sense for what the other was thinking or wanted to accomplish. AHP, on the other hand, still could not seem to get its rhythm, relying on cumbersome and time-consuming meetings to make even the simplest decisions. We were running dizzying circles around them.

PREPARING FOR BATTLE

I was deposing AHP's Dr. Fred Wilson, the medical monitor assigned to fen-phen. His deposition was going well, better than any of us had expected. He was a very likable man in his seventies, and his testimony was much more candid than that of younger witnesses who still had reason to protect their careers.

Halfway through Dr. Wilson's deposition, Charlie Ornstein, a reporter with *The Dallas Morning News* called. He wanted a quote about the decision that had just obliterated my nearly two million dollar breast implant judgment that had been pending in the Texarkana Court of Appeals. He must have assumed I already knew, but I did not. Now I was wishing I had let it go to voicemail.

Charlie got his answer, and I returned to Dr. Wilson, but my concentration was blown. It was hard to remember where I had left off. I referred to my notes, wracking my brain, but my mind was reeling. Charlie's unexpected news signaled the end of an era, one of the most important chapters of my career. One minute I was on top of the fen-phen world; moments later, my breast implant cases were trampled by a herd of judicial buffalo.

The appeal was a case we had previously won, an award of almost two million dollars. The defendant, 3M, appealed the ruling. I had continued to fight it alongside my fen-phen cases ever since. Now it was over and there was no longer anything I could do.

Almost all pharmaceutical liability cases involve a dispute about whether the drugs or device in question caused the plaintiff's injuries. And damages (the amount the judge or jury awards to the plaintiff) depend on it. The two million dollar breast implant judgment had just been wiped away because the Appeals Court ruled my causation evidence did not provide the necessary connection.

The ruling affected all personal injury cases in Texas, including fen-phen, putting them in the same boat as the implant cases. Fen-phen had been removed from the market almost a year earlier. There were still no scientific causation studies proving the drugs more than doubled the risk of getting heart valve disease when compared to the general, non-exposed population. Everyone involved eagerly awaited the inevitable publication of something—anything—that would scientifically steer the direction of the litigation one way or the other.

The next day, I was still reeling from the breast implant news. Robert took the lead questioning Dr. Joe Pittelli, a senior AHP scientist. We knew Dr. Pitteli's deposition probably would not yield much of significance in comparison to Dr. Wilson the day before, and we had not considered him an important witness in the grand scheme of things. At the same time, he was already on the schedule, so we had the attitude that we should just take his deposition and get it over with.

Dr. Pittelli must have sensed our indifference. He was not used to being unimportant; he was accustomed to being the most intelligent and revered man in the room. Perhaps that is why he volunteered the news that would position him as one of our most valued resources.

Dr. Pittelli boasted that, on September 10, *The New England Journal of Medicine* would publish a series of three important fen-phen articles.

A month later, *The New England Journal of Medicine* was waiting for me at the front of the medical school library. In it were articles authored by scientists from respected medical institutions such as Harvard, Georgetown, and Boston University, and there was even an editorial by Dr. Arthur Weyman, Professor of Cardiology at Duke University School of Medicine. They were precisely what the courts relied on to determine if certain scientific testimony should be allowed.

Dr. Weyman's two-page letter to the editor analyzed all three articles and offered his assessment: fen-phen could cause valve leakage when taken for at least ninety days.

The trio of articles became the cornerstone of most medical arguments in fen-phen cases involving heart valve leakage. The scientific hurdles that had proven insurmountable in breast implant litigation would not pose a problem in fen-phen.

PREPARING FOR BATTLE

🏛

Robert and I had attacked early in the recent depositions, yet it had been risky. We had taken almost twenty depositions and had accumulated and cataloged nearly two million documents. But AHP's defense team was becoming smarter, and soon our swashbuckling style would fail to surprise them. We needed a strategy that would catch the defense team off guard.

We moved the depositions to Philadelphia, and our friends from Houston took over with Robert nearby for support. I would work from the Dallas office.

In November, after hearing Robert brag about their impressively executed attack methods, I attended one of the Houston team's depositions. They had a high-tech war room set up in the bowels of the Philadelphia Four Seasons. In place of sofas were neatly labeled boxes of evidence stacked two-deep and as high as gravity would allow. Where there had once been luggage racks and wastebaskets, there were now full size computers on folding tables with printers, copiers, scanners, shredders, and fax machines. A maze of extension and power cords snaked between the workers, literally keeping them on their toes. Every electrical outlet in the room had been maxed out. A heavy-duty copier stood where the wear pattern on the carpet suggested a small sofa and coffee table had previously been.

A battalion of lawyers and paralegals were stationed there at all hours of the day and into the evening. They were in charge of files, exhibits, medical articles, and transcripts. And when something was needed down the street, they functioned like the tiny workings of a fine watch.

I sat next to Robert at the deposition the next morning, coffee in hand, four or five seats from the witness. The room there was as impressive as the setup the night before. It was all business, and as the first few questions were asked, I knew turning it over to Houston had been the right move.

I nudged Robert and whispered, "Those AHP guys must tremble at the sight of these cowboys every morning."

"Yep," he said even more quietly. We watched as one of the young attorneys from the night before wheeled in several heavy boxes of documents, much to the disliking of AHP's defense team. "They're wishing it was you and me alone down there in Dallas. We were nothing compared to the hell these Houston guys are putting 'em through!"

FIVE

FALSE START

WITH MOST OF our depositions complete, the Mary Perez case was scheduled for trial in February of 1999, in Morrilton, Arkansas, and Debbie Lovett in May in Canton, Texas. We were doing everything we could to get American Home Products in front of a jury quickly. The first fen-phen trial was sure to attract publicity. Being the first to verdict would attract new clients, a constant concern in any commission-based business. Most importantly, it would be big news, and staying newsworthy would force AHP to remain on the defensive.

In my struggle to take the lead, I also attracted another kind of attention—one I had not anticipated. AHP's legal team was scrutinizing my every move, waiting for me to make a mistake.

Any lawyer getting ready for a jury trial in a big case must be wary of the delicate nature of publicity. Those who attempt to try the case in the media could be faced with delays or a move to a remote venue. In early 1999, CBS News contacted me for their show *60 Minutes II*. They wanted my input on a story about fen-phen, so I agreed to help. This would give my firm a great deal of exposure, especially now that most in the medical community were convinced that fen-phen was, indeed, bad medicine. *The Fen-Phen Files* aired February 10. That evening, Leslie and I made drinks and ceremoniously peeled the cellophane off a brand new VHS tape. My hands shook as I wrote the title on the label and pressed it onto the cassette. I did not know if I was nervous about the show, afraid I would mess up the recording, or worried about what Leslie would think. She had become an important part of my life. I found myself wanting to impress her more and more, and she seemed to get a kick out of the increasing publicity. But the exposure also meant I spent more time working with each new client and saw her less, and I worried that she would become bored or resentful.

I tried to set the VCR to record, but my hands were shaking. Leslie took the remote control out of my hand, hit a couple of buttons and turned to flash me one of her "it'll be alright" smiles. I saw the record light, and my nervousness quickly disappeared.

In the segment, Mary, young and pretty with flashing eyes, appeared with her husband Tom and their little daughter. Mary was living with PPH, a lung disease with a grim prognosis. "Basically, they sent me home, told me to get my affairs together," she recalled, hopelessness bleeding through every word. Chances were her daughter would lose her mother before they could shop for makeup, prom dresses, or wedding gowns. Her husband's eyes welled up when he recounted the moment he realized something was wrong. "Right in the middle of the kitchen, she just about stumbled and fell," he recalled. "She grabbed herself, and she told me, she said, 'I feel like I just died for a split second.'"

A small hand tightened around my own, bringing me back to reality. Leslie related to Mary, having struggled with asthma all of her life. I was glad to have her there with me and pulled her closer.

One of the medical experts featured on the segment was Dr. Lewis Rubin, a physician and leading PPH medical researcher. He compared the famous *60 Minutes* ticking clock to the time bomb inside a PPH sufferer's chest. "The clock stops when the patient dies." No one is able to predict how much time someone with the disease has.

Narrator Vicki Mabrey described Mary's daily medical routine and her fears about how her illness affected her child. "So when Mary Perez found out she had a ticking clock, she hired Kip Petroff to sue Wyeth-Ayerst, the maker of fenfluramine, the first 'fen' in fen-phen."

Leslie squeezed my hand proudly as my face appeared onscreen in front of millions of viewers. "Petroff asked for all of Wyeth's internal documents on fen-phen, and this is what he got." For the first time outside of our North Texas circle, the world was seeing a remarkable image: our Fort Worth document depository and the seemingly insurmountable volumes of evidence. "Boxes and boxes of fen-phen files."

Dr. Sydney Wolfe, co-author of a book on the subject of consumer drugs, may have summarized it best: "If it saves your life, it's worth taking the chance. We don't have anything like that here. These drugs don't have evidence of long-term effectiveness. So you've got no long-term benefits, and some long-term risks."

The piece was a huge victory for the victims of fen-phen, but it was hard to revel in the glory knowing Mary and her family still had to deal with her illness and impending death. But *The Fen-Phen Files* would put pressure on AHP to take care of Mary Perez, make her life somewhat easier in the final days, and to care for her daughter after her mother's death.

Two days later, I was at the Dallas airport, on my way to Little Rock for a hearing on Mary's case, when I picked up a copy of *U.S. News and World Report*. The banner title stretched across the top of the front cover: "EXCLUSIVE: DANGEROUS DIET DRUGS." The Table of Contents under *Business and Technology* read: "Weight-loss wars: A spate of deaths among diet-drug users has prompted a raft of highly charged lawsuits." Mary Perez and I were the article's main subjects. News about fen-phen was everywhere.

🏛

The Little Rock hearing that afternoon was a general pretrial hearing that allowed AHP to formally challenge the science our side was counting on: that taking fen-phen could cause PPH and, in Mary's case, actually did. "General causation" (that the drugs were capable of causing this horrific disease) and "specific causation" (that the drugs actually caused the disease in Mary's case) were the legal terms used to describe the plaintiff's dual burden of proof. We needed the court to allow our experts to testify about both.

We pulled into the dirt parking lot at Ben Carruth's office building, which was more like a two-story country home than an office. Carruth was our local counsel on the Perez case. Once inside, his secretary handed me a copy of AHP's Motion for Continuance, catching me completely off guard. The article had just hit newsstands a day earlier. As "Exhibit A" to its motion, AHP was requesting that the Perez case be delayed for at least four more months.

🏛

Judge Danielson began the hearing with AHP's Fourth Motion for Continuance. Lyn Pruitt argued the motion for AHP. She alleged that I was single-handedly rigging the system, poisoning the jurors' minds, and denying her corporate citizen a fair trial. She strutted and pranced around the courtroom, occasionally pointing a scolding finger at me, and delighted in asking the judge for my head.

As convincing as her veil dance may have been, Judge Danielson denied the motion, in part because he said Conway County jurors did not pay much attention to the magazine or *60 Minutes II*. Besides, he could always reconsider if we learned otherwise during jury selection.

That denial must have been the straw that broke the camel's back. Just three days before trial, AHP offered Mary a settlement she simply could not refuse.

🏛

Now that Mary Perez's case was settled, it appeared mine would not be the first tried in the courtroom after all. It was a disappointment, but if anyone was going to beat me, I was glad it was going to be my pals Mike McGartland and Dan McDonald, and their client, Sandra Moore. My plan was to travel to Johnson County, Texas, to observe every day of the Sandra Moore trial, scheduled to begin in March 1999, in the county seat of Cleburne.

The Johnson County Courthouse is in the middle of the City of Cleburne, a small rural community an hour south of Dallas. Defense lawyers in breast implant litigation had avoided trials there because jurors tended to punish big business.

Bill Sims, lead counsel for AHP, had reason to feel confident that his client would be treated fairly—if he was allowed to try the case his way. He had been a lead plaintiff's lawyer in one of the largest jury verdicts in Johnson County history, which had resulted in a two hundred-eleven million dollar verdict against David's Supermarket, Inc. Sims owned a ranch in the heart of the county, and had a way of reminding folks that he was their neighbor.

Robert called a few days into arguments hoping to save me a trip to Cleburne. "That case is going to settle first thing tomorrow morning—if not tonight. They came up with four hundred thousand dollars today, and I don't think McGartland and company are going to push on with that much money on the table. If I were you, I wouldn't bother."

Despite Robert's warning, the courtroom junkie inside me needed its fix. Besides, I had been there to see the jury's reactions, and during two days of testimony, they had not appeared sympathetic to the plaintiff's case. I went anyway, and, as predicted, they settled that morning. As the jury filed out, they appeared even less sympathetic than the day before, which was a bit unnerving.

That afternoon, I began getting nervous about the fact that my case was now next. Unless it settled like Mary Perez and Sandra Moore, I would achieve my goal of being the first to go to verdict. I hoped the jury would be more sympathetic to my client, Debbie Lovett, than the Sandra Moore jury had appeared.

The Moore settlement meant that AHP's lawyers had a new trial calendar. The next case scheduled was Debbie Lovett vs. AHP, our case out east in Canton, Texas. I had almost six weeks to finalize preparations.

One day, shortly after the Moore settlement, I was leaving the law firm of Vinson and Elkins when I ran into Bill Sims. He was standing outside his office, which was right across from the conference room where I had just been examining expert witness materials.

"Hey, Kip. Good to see you." Bill smiled and invited me to join him for a minute.

"Their names are Fen and Phen," he beamed, once inside his office. He was pointing to a framed photo of two bulldogs. He tried to explain which was which, but they both looked the same to me.

I was more interested in his trial calendar. There were so many fen-phen cases, I assumed it was his way of tracking the entire trial circuit, but he explained that they were all part of his own personal calendar.

"Right now it's looking like your team and mine are going to spend some time together in Canton. The company rented a small house in town for me and my two dogs for the next six months, and they signed a one-year lease on an office building across from the courthouse."

It was then that I noticed that all the listings had the plaintiff's name and trial venue next to the start date on the calendar, but the two Canton cases were different. They both had the client and location like the others, but they also had my name. It was the only lawyer's name I could see.

In the past, I might have felt like this was an attempt to intentionally provoke me—the comments, the calendar, the ugly fen-phen dogs. But that was unlike Bill. He was the opposition in a high-powered case, but he was also a man of undeniable character.

"I really hope you're right," I replied sincerely. "I've been trying to pin your client down to trial settings for months now, but they keep squirming away."

Bill glanced toward the calendar. "You know all about your cases, Kip. I know the diagnosis, and that's about it. I get to make the arguments and put the witnesses on the stand, but other people handle everything else, and they're the ones who really know the cases." Then he paused and added, "It's probably too late for us to trade roles, but I kind of like your job better. You don't have to report to committees of other people who have never seen a courtroom but who want to offer all kinds of trial advice. I spend more time talking to executives about strategy than trying cases. Actually getting in the courtroom is going to be a whole lot more fun."

We walked toward the elevators. Bill was likable, even though it would soon be his job to try to defeat me. The elevator opened and I boarded. "See you around, Bill."

The door began to close when Bill put a large hand up to stop it. He leaned in and added, "The other thing I know, Kip, is that it will be a real pleasure trying a lawsuit against you and Kisselburgh. You two have done great things with this litigation in a short time, and you deserve the chance to be the first ones to get a verdict. I hope to God it's a defense verdict or a slap-in-the-face-lowball-plaintiff's verdict." He laughed and released the door, and as it was closing he added, "Should be fun trying a case against you two."

That brief conversation with Bill Sims played in my head for days. For whatever reason, AHP wanted to try these cases when they had settled Mary Perez and Sandra Moore. That concerned me. "Lovett/Petroff/Canton" and "Thornton/Petroff/Canton." Those words, written neatly on two squares six weeks apart on the large calendar in Sims' office, haunted me.

Bill Sims was a hell of a trial lawyer. He put people at ease, made friends with the enemy. Logic told me to distrust and dislike him, but that was impossible. I worried the jury would feel the same.

SIX

☰

A DEVASTATING BLOW

MID-APRIL MEETING in Tulsa was interrupted by a call from my paralegal, Melissa. "Kip. It's Leslie. She's been in a bad accident," she said.

"What? I'm sorry, it's ..." I inched toward a quiet corner, cupping my hand over the phone to channel the sound. "It's really busy in here. What did you say?"

"Leslie's been in a really bad wreck. She's at Presbyterian Hospital. Kip, you need to get home right away."

Leslie and I had known each other less than a year and had dated about eight months. She was fun, patient, and understanding. I loved spending time with her, but committing to love her had never even crossed my mind. We had just gotten to the point where we were talking about emotions and feelings; we agreed not to rush things. And now this.

When I arrived at Presbyterian, I learned Leslie had suffered a severe asthma attack while driving to a deposition and was trying to rush herself to the hospital when she crashed. Both lungs were punctured and collapsed.

Weeks earlier, as we watched Mary Perez on TV, I had comforted her, but now no one could. A machine breathed for Leslie, because she would never again be able to breathe for herself. The doctors explained that we needed to allow her to die in peace.

🏛

Prior to Leslie's accident, all I could think about was the trial a couple of weeks away. But at that moment, seeing her in a hospital bed with tubes in her mouth, hearing the incessant beeping of the heart monitor along with the rhythmic pumping of oxygen, and beholding the massive swelling of her pretty face, the trial seemed unimportant.

My heart was breaking. No amount of crying eased the pain, so I worked on upcoming cases to distract myself. But then some sound or smell or memory would shock me back into reality, and I was back at the hospital and Leslie was barely clinging to life. If I was going to make it through this, I had to stop feeling altogether.

People from the office came to offer their support and to bring me files to help pass the time and distract me. Still, I was getting further behind. I needed to make a decision, and I knew no one would blame me for asking for a delay. Then Leslie's mother handed me a *Texas Monthly Magazine*, just released and featuring my work. The journalist wrote, "He's Fen Phenomenal," saying I had pushed so hard I had put AHP "on the ropes." Leslie would have laughed about that, knowing I struggle with compliments. She would tell me to use my sadness to keep fighting.

Leslie Geer was on a ventilator for five days before her parents made the painful decision to let her die. She was buried April 26, 1999. She was only thirty years old.

🏛

A DEVASTATING BLOW

With my emotions completely suppressed, I focused on the mission ahead. But the tug-of-war between numbness and grief was constant. A fork with a tiny bit of lipstick the dishwasher had missed would send me into deep depression. That was how I went into jury selection for the Lovett trial. Our first attempt at seating a jury ended in a mistrial when the judge determined we lacked enough acceptable candidates. I blamed myself for failing to ask for a larger jury pool. My refusal to grieve had blown the start date of our trial. With my calendar cleared and nothing to distract me, it was time to put Leslie to rest. I took a short vacation to face the emotions I had ignored since the accident.

A few weeks later, we rescheduled Lovett and used the remainder of May to step up preparations, but June brought some frightening news. Word had it that Houston almost lost a primary pulmonary hypertension death case. This was the same disease that Mary Perez had and for which we had gotten a good settlement. Mary was still alive, but the lady in Houston had died. It should have been an easy win, a sure thing, but several of the jurors later stated that they had actually been leaning in favor of the defendants. Victory was not a guarantee.

I was weeks away from arguing a mild valve leakage case in Canton, one that had already had its share of bad luck. I had been so outspoken and confident; now my confidence seemed more like cockiness.

Muhammad Ali, back when he was still Cassius Clay, had famously taunted Sonny Liston for the heavyweight championship of the world, which prompted this message from Liston's manager: "I've flown 3,000 miles just to tell you Liston wants you. You've talked yourself into a title fight."

I, too, had talked big. I had taunted AHP, and now my name was tiny on its gigantic calendar. The fight was on.

SEVEN

FIGHT TIME

IN HIS LARGER-THAN-LIFE Colonel Sanders voice Lonnie stated, "I'm flattered that you and Robert would ask me to get involved in this trial, but I really don't think I could do anything that you two fine lawyers can't do yourselves. I've taught y'all everything I know, and I just don't see that I can add anything." Sincere modesty was part of Lonnie McGuire's southern charm.

In light of the previous mistrial, Robert and I had both agreed that hiring Lonnie, our former boss, was a smart idea. I was an Ohio boy, and Robert was from California. Although we had both successfully transplanted ourselves into Texas, we still had a way to go before either of us would be truly accepted into good ol' boy circles. Lonnie, with his string tie and comfortable drawl, was the real thing. He would be an asset.

"Not true, Lonnie. You helped me select a jury in Upshur County on our last breast implant trial, and you could also help us in Canton," I encouraged. Lonnie was sincerely flattered that his two protégés would want to hire him for such a potentially significant case, but he seemed just as sincere when he rattled off the reasons why he would be declining our request.

"Alright, I can understand not wanting to try the entire case with us, but how about letting us hire you by the day to help us pick the Lovett jury?" His silence was encouraging, so I pressed on. "If you still don't want to try the case after the jury is in the box, then you can go home whenever you want."

"Why, I can't pass up an offer like that, especially when it comes from my two favorite young lads. You just let me know what you want me to do and what time the train leaves for Canton. I'll be on it." With the addition of Lonnie McGuire for the jury selection phase, our tiny Texas trial team was starting to look mighty.

On the morning of Monday, July 12, 1999, Bill Sims watched from the top step outside the courtroom as the bailiff herded in potential jurors. He greeted me warmly and spoke quietly and slowly once he was sure no jurors could see us talking. "I won't be trying this case after all. Some attorneys up in Jersey are pushing a medical monitoring suit. They want to get free echos for every fen-phen user in the state, and now the company wants me there instead of here. So I'm here to help with jury selection, and then I'm on a plane to New York."

Bill was the best lawyer they had for this trial, so it was a relief to see him going somewhere else—anywhere but here. "Gonna miss you, but I'm sure we'll have a chance again somewhere along the way. Have fun up north," I said, shaking Bill's hand as we entered the courtroom.

With Lonnie aboard, we avoided another mistrial and selected our jury by the end of the first day. The Jurors' Oath was administered, and they were dismissed with instructions to return the next morning. It was a small victory, but we were all relieved to have overcome the hurdle that had tripped us up last time. For better or worse, the trial was about to begin. The battle against Goliath was on.

The large courtroom seemed oddly empty to me, even more so

as everyone busied themselves with preparations. I felt conspicuous without my own busy work, so I was relieved when Pat Spruiell took the seat next to me. Pat was local co-counsel and had allowed us to use his office. He looked around to make sure no one was listening, scooted his chair a little closer, and said, "We got a good looking jury. Much better than the one I saw last week in this court."

"I hope so," I replied.

"They'll take care of that little girl if you can prove half the things you told 'em today. In fact," he added, "I don't think the drug company will let you take a verdict in this case."

"Oh, I can prove everything, but I don't think AHP cares," I said. "The home office has decided to take this case all the way to verdict, and they mean it." They had yanked their previous offer of a quarter-million dollars. "Guess I pissed them off or something. They haven't talked settlement since last week, and they say they're not going to."

"They'll try," Pat added, sounding sure of himself.

The little girl Pat referred to was our client, Debbie Lovett, a sweet thirty-four-year old manicurist, wife, and mother. After the birth of her second son, she struggled to lose weight, so she began taking fen-phen in October 1995. She learned about the drug cocktail from a *Reader's Digest* article that had helped popularize the magic pills. She took the combination on and off for about a year and a half, and like so many others, she lost the weight, though only temporarily.

Unlike most users, however, Debbie received an echocardiogram both before and after taking the drugs. Her pre-fen-phen echo showed no sign of aortic valve damage, but the echo performed afterward showed clear aortic valve damage—the kind of damage directly associated with the diet drug. We hoped to prove to the jury that only fen-phen could be responsible for the change that occurred between the two echos. But we would be up against a powerhouse that wanted nothing more than to prove us wrong.

🏛

To say that Robert Kisselburgh was a good trial partner for the first fen-phen case is like saying Tarzan might be a good man to have with you your first day in the jungle. He easily managed dozens of volumes of information. I knew the sound bites and one-liners, but Robert was the key to painting a large, well-defined picture that would make sense to the jury.

We were in the courtroom by seven thirty on the morning opening statements were scheduled to begin. Robert was there early to tend to various and numerous audiovisual issues, and I was there to get psyched up for my opening statement.

A reporter named Alicia Mundy was there doing research on fen-phen. She had interviewed me in the weeks before the trial, which resulted in the magazine article that outraged AHP's lawyer on the eve of the Mary Perez trial. She thought the fen-phen fiasco would make a good book, and I was certainly happy to help with that, too. But having Alicia Mundy hanging around had become too much for the rest of my team. They seized my phone and grounded me from the media until after the trial. Robert warned, "You'd better be careful, Kip. One day that media you crave is going to jump up and bite you in the ass!"

🏛

Finally the trial began. My job was to paint a picture the jury would understand, so I started at the beginning: At seventeen, Debbie Lovett experienced heart palpitations, which is another way of saying her heart was beating too fast. Her cardiologist at the time conducted an echocardiogram and thought he noticed a mitral valve prolapse (a small bulge in one of the valves on the left side of the heart) and a slight regurgitation (backflow of blood), so he put her on medication. A slight mitral regurgitation is actually fairly normal, rarely progresses, and is generally asymptomatic. Years later, Debbie had a follow-up echocardiogram with a new doctor who said her heart looked normal. He did not detect a prolapse as the first doctor had. Then, after taking Pondimin and experiencing some unusual heart palpitations, Debbie had yet another echocardiogram. This time it was interpreted as moderate regurgitation in both the mitral and aortic valves. Aortic leakage is the type of valve damage generally associated with Pondimin use. Our argument was that Debbie's previous heart problem could not have caused the aortic valve problem and that Pondimin had to be to blame.

We called our witnesses who talked about the drugs' defects, how the drugs caused heart problems, how those problems were either misinterpreted or hidden from the FDA and consumers. They explained how the product recall came only after public pressure forced the company to come clean.

We played clips from our extensive collection of video depositions during strategic moments in the trial. The jury saw Dr. Wilson admitting that AHP should have warned of the dangers of valve leakage before Debbie ever took the drugs. We also exposed AHP's under-the-radar promotion of the fen-phen cocktail using scare tactics, such as exaggerating the obesity crisis with inflated statistics.

Next we focused on AHP's motive: money. Pondimin's sales had skyrocketed after doctors began pushing the drug combo. Profit was the goal, not patient safety or well-being. Issues such as medical monitoring, long-term use, and the traditional black box would have warned users of serious risks. In Pondimin's case, these were secondary to the company's profit margin.

The witness who may have provided the most important testimony was Dr. Jo Alene Dolan. Dr. Dolan was not a medical doctor, but she was one of the people assigned by AHP to serve as medical monitor for Pondimin during a time when there was confusion about who actually filled that important role.

Dolan, known amongst her peers as the "Queen of Redux," was involved in the ghostwriting of medical articles. AHP paid twenty thousand dollars for one such article, which resulted in a medical journal claiming that obesity was a long-term medical problem and that long-term pharmacotherapy management was the recommended solution. AHP was restricted from publishing the article itself due to numerous FDA regulations. Using an independent author allowed it to make such claims legally, but the breach of ethics was undeniable.

The Queen of Redux also testified about the S.W.A.T. Team that had been organized to resist stronger FDA warnings for Pondimin and the soon-to-be-approved Redux. She attempted to explain the confusion around the medical monitor position, and also why a multi-billion dollar company used temporary employees for safety surveillance despite the drug's ballooning sales.

Two weeks later, we wrapped. AHP would begin presenting their arguments the following Monday. We were surprised to find out their first witness would be Debbie's own cardiologist, Dr. J. Edward Rosenthal, whom we had purposefully avoided.

Dr. Rosenthal appeared for trial Monday morning looking a bit out of place in East Texas in his expensive suit. After reciting very impressive credentials, he proceeded to deconstruct Debbie's case. He argued that Debbie's aortic valve damage was a natural progression of her original mitral valve problem and insisted she had a pre-existing mitral valve prolapse that contributed to it.

I reminded Dr. Rosenthal of the testimony of the other experts who explained that the two types of valve damage were not related. He disagreed, asserting that he had greater experience. Dr. Rosenthal's echo of Debbie's heart had been lost or erased years earlier, so there was no way to compare his study to the one her internist had performed.

Robert seemed convinced that the case suffered irreparable damage as a result of Dr. Rosenthal's testimony, even though I thought I had successfully cross-examined him. "I don't know how to say this other than by getting right to the point," Robert began, rarely a good sign. "We have to settle this case. I can already hear AHP's lawyers repeating over and over how 'the only cardiologist who ever placed hands on Debbie testified that there was nothing wrong with her that she didn't already have before she took fen-phen. It's just a natural progression of a pre-existing disease.' It's over, and we need to settle for whatever we can, or we're going to end up with nothing."

The drug company needed a winning verdict as much as I wanted one. A win for them would weaken the thousand other cases already scheduled to go to court. It might also deter claimants from going forward with their cases. A win for us would have the opposite effect, fueling even more victories and boosting plaintiffs' confidence.

"I've been bad-mouthing AHP and bragging about my great pretrial depositions to anyone who would listen," I reminded him. "I busted their balls, and now it's time for payback. They're not going to let up."

"You don't know that. At least talk to them," Robert urged.

"I can't just go up to them now with hat in hand and ask them to pay me enough to cover my expenses so I can finance my next trial against them." I was at the end of my rope and needed Robert to loosen the noose rather than tighten it. "I can't initiate that conversation. I won't."

Robert finally conceded, reluctantly. The topic of settlement was never mentioned again in this case—not by Robert, not by AHP, and certainly not by me.

American Home Products continued its arguments saying it was a successful pharmaceutical company with a good reputation. Why would it risk that for just one drug? And after all, they had the FDA's approval.

In an effort to deflect blame from the company, AHP instead focused on Debbie, her pre-existing condition, and the fact that she appeared healthy and symptom-free. Debbie's own doctor testified that our expert cardiologist, Dr. Waenard Miller, was greatly exaggerating her valve leakage.

AHP admitted its Pondimin labeling was incomplete and outdated, but maintained it was sufficient and in keeping with FDA standards. Repeating their well-worn mantra, they asserted that obesity was a medical issue responsible for hundreds of thousands of deaths and illnesses—despite their inability to support the claims.

Bill Sims even returned from up north to put company official Dr. Ginger Constantine on the stand. She testified that the drug company jumped on the heart valve problem immediately, flying to Minnesota in a snowstorm to investigate just days after receiving the first cluster of reports from the Mayo Clinic.

The jury showed no signs that they were leaning one way or the other. Before Bill Sims came to AHP's rescue, they had appeared moved by my simple portrait of a sweet country girl persecuted by the rich, greedy drug company. But Bill was charismatic and could change the jurors' minds.

After Constantine's testimony, Sims left Canton with the rest of AHP's A team. With the B Team back in place, I could use the upcoming closing arguments to continue painting my masterpiece.

FIGHT TIME

Closing arguments are a lawyer's final opportunity to make a solid case by summarizing and explaining the evidence. It is also the first time since opening statements that the jury is directly addressed. Sometimes jurors will have made up their minds early, and nothing will change that. The Lovett jury was different. After Sims' departure, I sensed, perhaps because I wanted to, that they were all still weighing the evidence.

Robert and I agreed to split our time. I would concentrate on company negligence, corporate sloppiness and laziness, and medical issues. Robert would focus on company deceit, marketing, corporate greed, and the unethical, albeit legal, ghostwriting.

My argument felt mechanical and business-like. I discussed the echocardiograms, drug usage, and how AHP should have given Debbie's prescribing physician more complete information. I reminded the jury that Pondimin was responsible for the changes in Debbie's echos. Video clips from depositions confirmed that AHP either missed or ignored obvious warning signs.

Robert began his closing argument by grabbing a full and heavy box of AHP's internal documents that had been admitted into evidence and slamming it on our table. It worked. Jurors stirred in their seats as Robert removed the lid.

The defense team whispered nervously.

This was Robert's chance to tell the jurors and the world what he and his law clerks—and later the Houston lawyers—had uncovered in the twenty-three months since the drugs were removed from the market. Almost two years of tedious, inglorious work was bottled up inside him, and he channeled it into one climactic, impassioned indictment of the company's financial motivation. He had no notes, nor did he need an outline. Robert held up document after document, explaining how it all fit together into one big, greedy corporate quest. He showed charts of early lackluster sales followed by a drastic forty-fold spike in profits after AHP began promoting the drug combination.

Robert had the jury excited, curious, and even angry. It took a mere ten minutes to summarize how the company put profits ahead of people as they made many hundreds of millions of dollars off customers' lack of information.

He had been living with those documents for almost two years and knew them like no one else. Like a tornado, Robert's argument was a hot rush of wind that stirred the fen-phen debris into a powerful, choking cloud the jury simply could not ignore.

Brian Johnson spoke first for the defense. My stomach was in nervous knots, but it escalated to pure nausea when I heard him say, "I'm sorry that she's been dragged through a lawsuit by some people, and she's been used and misled. I think it leaves a stain on my profession that I'm not very proud of." He further suggested I was playing "litigation lotto," using Debbie to try to get rich rather than looking out for her best interest.

Robert must have sensed my anger. He leaned over and whispered, "Stay calm."

Then Joe Piorkowski took his turn speaking on behalf of the drug company. He tried to convince the jury that we had bullied Dr. Wilson into admitting that AHP should have warned about heart valve leakage long before Debbie and millions like her ever took fen-phen.

Robert tactfully avoided calling the defense counsel outright liars by introducing to the jury a recent dictionary.com Word of the Day: *obfuscate.*

Not me. "I'm not going to say *obfuscate*," I began in rebuttal. "I'm going to say lie, because that is what happened here. *Lie*—I've never once used that in a courtroom to refer to a lawyer's closing statement, but a lie is what you've had." I looked each juror in the eye as my final statements brought the first fen-phen case to an end. "So when you get back there, and you deliberate on this case, keep in mind that you have the power in this first fen-phen case in the history of our country—

you have the power to tell them *you had better get it right next time*." I lowered my voice. "And I know you'll do right. You'll come out of here with your heads held high and look us in the eye and say, 'Yeah, we did it. We did it. We're going to make that company pay and think *twice* before they jeopardize the safety of the American public.'"

Was I the only one hearing my own deafening heartbeat? Closing arguments had unleashed a torrent of unexpected fury. I took my seat, drew a slow, deep breath, and pushed back three months of suppressed tears.

"Ladies and gentlemen," Judge Wallace stated in the juror's direction. "Now it's your turn. So will you please retire to the jury room and deliberate until you've reached a verdict."

Everyone stood as the jurors filed out.

The closing of the jury room door after final arguments is the symbolic end of the trial. It is usually a time when the lawyers shake hands and congratulate one another on a well-tried case. It was difficult to shake the two hands that had attacked my honor just moments earlier, but I did, and for the first time in my professional career—in my entire life—I felt dirty.

EIGHT

KNOCKOUT

THE LOVETT JURY reached their verdict just before noon on their third day of deliberations. Just as we had three and a half weeks earlier, we filed into the courtroom. Judge Wallace took his place, and after the usual formalities, he began. "I know that there has been a lot of stress in this trial, but please don't anyone say anything or shake your head or give any indication of whether you agree or disagree with this jury's verdict." And then, as if forecasting trouble, he added, "They did not ask to come down here."

The jury entered the quiet courtroom, took their seats, and shifted uncomfortably, as if they sensed we had been talking about them.

The charge is a series of pre-determined questions outlined before the deliberations. The jury is asked to answer the questions in a charge based on their interpretation of both sides' presentations. Other than the sounds made by the two speakers and the ticking away of the court reporter's steno machine, the room was absolutely silent.

As the judge started reading aloud, the stress Robert had been under the past several months bubbled to the surface. His breathing became labored and then took on a stuttering pattern.

Then, Judge Wallace read the first question. "Did the negligence, if any, of those named below proximately cause the injury in question?"

Debbie Lovett? *No.*

American Home Products? *Yes.*

Robert's breathing became more punctuated. The more he tried to quell the excitement, the harder it was for him to breathe normally. I tried hard to ignore him, very aware that I was teetering on the edge of an emotional purging.

The judge continued. "Was there a marketing defect in Pondimin?"

Yes.

"Was there a design defect in Pondimin?"

Yes.

The fourth question and answer found AHP one hundred percent negligent and Debbie Lovett not at all.

Debbie was sobbing. The uncertainty was gone, and she relinquished control of her emotions. It became difficult to continue taking notes. What the judge said next made me drop my pen.

"What sum of money, if paid now in cash, would fairly and reasonably compensate Debbie Lovett for her injuries that resulted from the occurrence in question?"

Past physical pain and mental anguish, fifty thousand dollars. *Future physical pain and mental anguish,* five hundred thousand dollars. *Future loss of earning capacity,* three hundred thousand dollars. *Past physical impairment,* five hundred thousand dollars. *Future physical impairment,* one million dollars. *Past and future medical care,* one million-twelve thousand dollars.

On top of that, punitive damages—those meant to send a message to the company that what they did was wrong—were twenty million dollars. The total amount of damages totaled $23,362,000, almost one hundred times what we had been willing to settle for just days earlier.

We had won, and we had won big.

We exited the courtroom into a mob of reporters. We made our statement, but they wanted more. We tried to answer their questions, but the noise became deafening. An escape across the grassy commons area to Pat Spruiell's office was not enough. The microphones, cameras, and notepads were on our heels.

We ducked into Pat's conference room, caught our breath, and collapsed into the silence. Pat's secretary poked her head in, grinning widely. "Um, I've got Dan Rather on line one and Katie Couric on line two," she giggled. Not one of us moved. We sat there, laughing, until Robert finally stood.

"We did it, Tiger," he smiled proudly.

I reached an arm around Debbie and gave her a big squeeze. "We did it."

Robert conducted an interview with *National Public Radio* in the car on the way back to Dallas that afternoon, and I interviewed with Dan Rather by satellite in Las Colinas just outside of Dallas that evening. Robert, Debbie, and her mother and I then flew to New York to appear on *Good Morning America* on Monday morning.

An urgent note from one of the *Good Morning America* producers was waiting for me at the front desk of the hotel. *This cannot be good news*, I thought. I was right.

"We can only have one of the attorneys on the show," she informed me. In other words, one of us, either Robert or I, was off. He looked disappointed, but he was mouthing that it was okay if I went on without him.

"Sorry," I told her. "We're a team. Either both attorneys do it, or we're all three out." It was a gamble I hoped would pay off.

"We've picked up legal analyst Jeffrey Toobin," she explained, "And we have to have Ms. Lovett, so there's just not room for both of you." Silence. "You understand, right?"

"No. We're a team."

Robert was pleading with me to just do the show without him, but this was a once in a lifetime chance.

"That's a shame," I said. "We were really looking forward to doing your show. I guess you'll have to find someone else to fill our spot, because Robert and I are a team. We go on together or we don't go on at all."

The *Good Morning America* limousine picked all of us up from our hotel at four forty-five the next morning. We were in the dressing room having coffee, bagels, and fruit by five o'clock. Debbie, Robert, and I took turns getting our hair and makeup done as we waited for our cue to go on air as a team.

George Stephanopoulos was also slated to appear that morning for an unrelated story. He sat in stony silence shooting disapproving looks at some hippie crewmembers who were raiding the bagels. He never even once glanced at Debbie in her pretty Sunday dress. I felt a little sad for her. I'm sure she would have struck up a conversation, had it not been for the big city's unapproachable ambassador.

None of it—George, the hippies, or the food—could break my concentration. This would be live, and I was trying to stay calm so I would look somewhat intelligent on national television.

It was only after the interview that I learned that the hippies had not been with the crew. They were The Moody Blues, one of the greatest rock bands of my generation. Robert knew all along, but he also knew my fascination with rock bands and kept his secret so I would stay focused.

We survived the interview, picked up our complimentary VHS copies, and then went straight to Fox News for an on-camera interview. Robert, Debbie, and her mom then headed back to Dallas. I waited around until noon for a half-hour interview on CNN's *Burden of Proof.* Robert had his fill of the spotlight and skipped the final interview to get home to his family.

Monday evening, I grabbed *The Wall Street Journal* and *USA TODAY*, because they were just then scheduled to carry the Friday afternoon verdict. In an interview, I had told the *Journal* reporter we only had fifty clients. I was amused to see he had used his creative license to report that we had one hundred.

I wish we had a hundred, I thought. *Heck, I wish we had a thousand!*

NINE

PROPOSALS FOR
MARRIAGE & MONEY

THE FIRST FEW months after the Lovett verdict were like a dream come true. We were given the opportunity of a lifetime, and we made the most of it. Of course, we knew the amount of the verdict was going to be reduced by the appeals court because of Texas' strict tort reform laws. The way they are written, it is nearly impossible to sustain a punitive damage verdict big enough to send a message to a wealthy company. We took comfort knowing ours was just one of many to come.

As expected, AHP requested a new trial and was gearing up for a lengthy appeal. We soon settled for much less than the twenty-three million the jury awarded, but it was still a fair and impressive amount.

I bragged shamelessly to everyone—clients, lawyers, reporters— about what we were doing and how we were doing it. My goal was the same as it had always been: convince the clients with good cases to hire us and convince the lawyers with good cases to refer them to us. After Lovett, it got easier. We had credibility.

"Only the Statute of Limitations," I bragged, "could ever put an end to our new case inventory." Then, as if to rain on our parade, AHP announced that it was agreeing to pay roughly four billion dollars to settle the fen-phen controversy almost exactly two years after the drugs were removed from the market and just six weeks after we had nailed them with the Lovett verdict. The front page headline in the *Dallas Morning News* on September 22, 1999, read: "Millions could get testing, money in fen-phen deal: Drug maker set to pay $4 billion."

Despite our verdict, clients in the Nationwide Settlement with Debbie Lovett's medical condition would only receive six thousand dollars or up to ten thousand dollars for medical services. There were future benefits available if the condition worsened significantly. That was enough for me to know the deal was not for most of my clients, so I vocalized my opposition loudly from the beginning.

I had begun conducting and appearing as a guest speaker at fen-phen seminars before our Canton case. With the Lovett verdict, seminars seemed like a great way to forge ahead. When I would attend as a guest speaker, Michael Fishbein was often on the program as well. Fishbein, along with his partner Arnold Levin, had been appointed co-chair of the MDL. They had negotiated the deal with AHP, and now they were responsible for selling the settlement to others, a job Fishbein took very seriously. At seminars, Fishbein would proudly explain the settlement with charts and graphs. In the settlement, Debbie Lovett would have received only six thousand dollars. Diligent lawyers willing to put a little effort into their cases could get far more money for most of their clients. My pitch was controversial, and the journalists lapped it up eagerly.

Seminars were also a great place to grandstand. I compared Fishbein's deal to a birthday card from Grandma: before reading the sentimental stuff, look for the money. Throwing up my empty hands, I would ask, "Where's the cash?" This always got a good laugh from the audience—but not Fishbein.

Joking aside, the agreement's payment structure did not make sense. It paid people with mitral valve conditions substantially more than those with similar percentages of aortic leakage. Those with mild aortic valve leakage, which should have been the focus because it was more likely to have been caused by fen-phen, received very little money.

Fishbein would counter that this was the deal the defendant had come up with, and who was he to look a gift horse in the mouth? It did not matter to him who got the money or why the drug company was willing to hand over so much. In truth, Fishbein was entitled to a percentage of every case claimed under the settlement whether it was fair or not. At the same time, he had to be careful not to "bust the Trust" or disappoint the drug company. His balancing act rarely put the clients' interests first.

Another flaw was the promise of free medical testing for millions. If it happened, it would be an incredible benefit to bestow upon the drugs' users, considering how many there were. But Wyeth's legal and financial teams would probably warn against doing anything that could potentially diagnose valve leakage in tens of thousands of asymptomatic former customers—every one of whom would then be eligible for a large claim. Best-case scenario, this could cost the drug company as little as three billion; worst-case scenario, they could be subject to paying out more than twenty or thirty billion dollars. So, on top of the cost of the promised testing, the drug company was looking at a settlement with a potential price tag anywhere from nine billion dollars to thirty-three billion dollars. This was incentive enough for them to hope few people had their free echos.

Then, in November, the class action received another blow that added to its mounting problems. *The Philadelphia Inquirer* published a powerful article describing a controversial secret pact. It said the MDL would recommend that Judge Bechtle, the federal judge assigned to this class action, legally conclude that fen-phen valve disease was not latent (or dormant). They had apparently also agreed that "mild heart-valve problems do not impair a person's daily activities." Victims' claims were in danger of being trivialized or denied completely, not because of the nature of the claim itself, but due to the backroom negotiations between the corporate bully that pushed the dangerous drugs and the group of lawyers supposedly advocating on the victims' behalves.

Even mildly injured claimants would still have the option of suing for punitive damages, and, like Debbie, they could receive fair recoveries in court. That would be the way to go. But future claimants would have their hands tied if they did not opt out of the settlement in time because of the pact. If attorneys bought into the MDL's plan, the people they represented would be victimized again and again.

Robert and I were learning class actions on the job, so we had no idea why the MDL asked us to meet with them. Since the Lovett verdict, a lot of people had wanted to meet with us. Maybe that was the case with John Cummings and Stan Chesley, two of the co-chairs of the MDL Plaintiffs' Management Committee.

They explained that a significant bargaining tool in the $4.8 billion deal had been my Lovett verdict. They even told me that the word "Lovett" (it is pronounced luh-*vet*, but they mispronounced it *luv*-it) had become a noun and was used in the rhetorical question to AHP: "How many 'luv-its' can your company handle before it realizes this is a reasonable settlement?"

Cummings and Chesley invited me to join and support the MDL. We were flattered but suspected there were ulterior motives. If they could get me to subscribe to their get-rich-quick plan, I would have to stop attacking the Settlement Agreement publicly. Their charm tactics might have worked if I had been attacking it for attention or some sort of financial gain. But that simply was not the case. It was a ridiculous settlement for many reasons, and plaintiffs' attorneys, especially those representing aortic leakage cases, needed to know the truth.

Instead of joining the MDL, we filed a petition to intervene so that we could claim a fee for our work. I was feeling bold, and after all, they said our Lovett verdict had been an important bargaining tool. Attorneys often claim fees for their work if it provided a significant common benefit for others trying similar cases. Asking for such a fee was always done in advance, before the work was complete, but never afterwards as we had decided to do, and our hotheaded request was denied.

Ironically, the day after we signed the petition to intervene, an F-2 tornado hit downtown Fort Worth, killing five and injuring a hundred more. It would have been worse if not for the timing of the storm, which hit the business district after most employees had gone home for the day. The Bank One building, home of Mike McGartland's offices and our extensive document depository, was badly damaged. McGartland and his staff were unharmed and easily relocated, but millions of fen-phen documents were lost when the depository basement filled with floodwaters.

The tornado was an eerie omen, a reminder that everything—all our hard work and accomplishments—could all be blown away in an instant.

After Leslie's death, the hurt I felt became so intense that I had turned off the ability to have romantic feelings altogether. I still felt—anger, excitement, and even lust—but nothing that compared to the closeness she and I had built. As time went on, the emotional tap slowly turned, and I began feeling again. I dated a little, but it was still difficult to allow myself to truly care for another woman. A woman would have to be very special to win my heart.

Dana Clark was a receptionist for a one-man law firm, Chris Economou. The Tulsa lawyer represented the prescribing doctor in one of my cases. I was in town to take the doctor's deposition. Dana greeted us when we walked into the office. Her hand was cool, and when she slowly pulled it away, the softness of her skin stayed with me. She was tall, thin, and blonde, and the way she walked reminded me of one of those blonde bombshell actresses from the movies. Stunning. Her perfume lingered on my hand, and I was reminded of her each time it would make its way to my nose. I nervously flirted with her throughout the day and finally worked up the courage to ask if I could call her the next time I was in town. I assumed she was married to some bodybuilder and would say no, but to my surprise, she was single and agreed. I would have to wait to take her on a date until my case was finalized, but knowing she would be there to smile at me when I walked through the door made me eager to return.

At the time I met Dana, I was working on the case of a cardiovascular nurse who became faint while at work. She had valve surgery at the Mayo Clinic at the hands of one of the surgeons who co-wrote the original Mayo Clinic fen-phen article. Hers was a key case because it allowed me to take depositions of two of the leading Mayo Clinic physicians. But her case was key for another reason. It had been her case I was working on when I learned of Leslie's accident a year earlier. Now, in the same town and on the same mission, I was falling for Dana while wrapping up the nurse's case.

I liked Dana a lot, in a very similar way to how I cared for Leslie. I loved how Dana had simple tastes. She was happiest when she was playing with my dogs or tinkering in the yard. She did not drink much herself, but she didn't seem to mind my drinking and was even happy to drive when I'd had too much. At the time we dated, I was between publicity, and I missed the attention. Dana turned heads, and with her on my arm, I felt like I was back in the spotlight.

I held onto Dana with everything I had. When that seemed

inadequate, I held on tighter by proposing marriage. I had been too distracted to commit to Leslie before she died; that could not happen again. We were engaged after dating just two months, and three months after that we were married.

🏛

The class action settlement proposal was made official in the fall of 1999. Those who remained in the class action settlement would then be known as Matrix clients because they fit on the payment matrix or grid. Those who chose to opt out, thereby still maintaining their right to punitive damages, would either go to trial, or with luck, settle their cases separately. Those who stayed in could opt out later, but they could not seek punitive damages if they did.

As expected, Judge Bechtle's written opinion was consistent with the side agreement mentioned in *The Philadelphia Inquirer*. It would be a long time before some future litigants would fully realize how severely their hands were tied as a result.

We settled all our cases in January 2001, marking the end of what we would later refer to as Round One of fen-phen. At the time, I had no idea there would be a Round Two.

ROUND TWO

TEN

BATTLE WEARY

A SETTLEMENT INVOLVING a thousand sick clients takes months to finalize. There are sometimes factors that can muddy up a clear case like divorces, deaths, probate, taxes, medical liens, and bankruptcies. And sometimes multiple factors can bog down a single case, sucking it up like quicksand. Robert spent months cleaning up every issue on each client's file, collecting the necessary signatures, filing the claims, recording the checks, dispensing payments to clients and co-counsel, and eventually, *finally*, settling each case.

Then, at age 42, Robert informed me that he was retiring from the practice of law. He was experiencing burnout, and after the circus tricks he and I had performed in Round One, and the tediousness of the settlement details, he feared Round Two would bore him. Instead of all the media attention and court battles, I was surprised and a bit envious to learn he planned to get his master's degree in history and become a teacher.

Robert and I had been a great team. It would take two or three people to replace him, but there was no rush. Fen-phen had been challenging, but maybe it was time for a change. I had a beautiful new wife who would probably appreciate it if I spent more time at home, and the pain in my back had become crippling. I scheduled back surgery and used the recovery time to weigh my Round Two options.

Round Two was a siren's song, seducing me to return, just as the sirens lured sailors onto the jagged rocks. Ego was also a factor. My work from Round One would almost certainly continue to be used in Round Two, and I could not stand the thought of some inexperienced attorney fumbling around with my depositions, mishandling evidence, carelessly misinterpreting data, or mispronouncing witnesses' names. I was irked at the thought of reporters quoting someone else or having some imposter answer my questions at seminars and letting wet-behind-the-ears lawyers get rich off my work.

Alicia Mundy's book, *Dispensing with the Truth,* was receiving excellent reviews, and I could not wait to get my hands on a case of books so I could send copies out to everyone I knew. Robert and I were two of her main characters, but Alex MacDonald got top billing. His client, Mary Linnen, had died young and quite horrifically. Mundy told Mary's story with honesty and compassion and Debbie Lovett's story with great attention to detail. Stories like these need protagonists, and while we were just doing our jobs, Mundy's gift for words made heroes of Alex, Robert, and me.

I read Mundy's book while I recovered from back surgery. Reading about myself as a character in an exciting story made it hard to be patient. I attacked my physical therapy with enthusiasm and was back at work before anyone thought it was possible. As far as I was concerned, the fen-phen fight was not over.

In Round Two, I began to represent settlement cases, also known as grid or Matrix cases. We interchangeably called them that because they fit onto a grid-like diagram called a matrix. There were a number of factors that determine which matrix a client went onto and then where he or she fit on that particular one. The A Matrix was for claimants with no pre-existing factors, and the B Matrix was for those with one or more reduction factors. Clients on the A Matrix were paid five times more than those on B. Once on a Matrix, other considerations included age, duration of exposure to fen-phen, and severity.

I accumulated many more Matrix cases in Round Two because the nature of the Settlement Agreement allowed us to be less discerning. We were selective with the cases we accepted in Round One because we thought that we might have to prove in court that each client's condition resulted from fen-phen usage. However, we were not required to prove anything in Round Two; the client simply had to fit onto one of the grids. The Settlement Agreement promised to provide a final determination of each complete claim within no more than one hundred-twenty days of filing. This looked like a sure way to keep my firm's employees busy.

In Round One, I settled a thousand cases for more money than I had ever seen or ever thought I would see in my lifetime. Prior to this, having never really had wealth, I can honestly say I was acting out of a desire to practice law and to bring justice to my clients. But Round Two's low-hanging fruit was going to be picked by someone, so why not do the picking myself? Since I had laid the groundwork, I figured I had just as much right to it as anyone else. It was easy money—too easy to let go.

By the end of June 2002, due to about a hundred deals with law firms across the country, I had more than twenty thousand fen-phen clients.

☷

Unlike Round One, Round Two required extensive dealings with the AHP Settlement Trust. A trust is a fully staffed legal organization that administers class action settlement claims. It is responsible for both ensuring deserving claimants are paid and for policing funds so that no money is squandered. The Trust's promise of free echocardiograms had been nonsense, considering the limited amount of time and the millions of claimants who could potentially enroll. The math simply did not add up, and everyone but the Trust seemed to know it.

Before the screening period had even officially begun, potential clients came to me with stories about how the Trust was giving them the run around. They were put on hold for long periods of time, left messages that were never returned and had spent too much time waiting. Others felt the Trust doctor was rude or disinterested in their case, and some who actually received free echos claimed that they never received a report or a chance to visit with a doctor about the findings.

The screening period officially began January 3, 2002. It marked the limited time during which everyone who planned to make a claim had to receive echocardiograms. It would end at midnight 365 days later on January 3, 2003.

☷

Nancy Robinson started taking fen-phen in mid-1997 and lost fifty pounds in less than three months. She received her third prescription on September 12, 1997. That was three days before AHP announced a nationwide recall. The news would not reach Nancy until after she filled and consumed much of the prescription. Then her doctor called to warn her to stop taking the drugs due to "previously undisclosed health risks," and when she stopped, she quickly gained back the weight. Rather than hiring an attorney, Nancy got her free echo. But when she inquired about the results, she was told to be patient. While waiting, patiently, Nancy suffered a massive heart attack. The Trust sent her for another free echo, but after being left in the dark again, she finally hired an attorney who subsequently hired my firm. But her nightmare got worse. After surgeons discovered severe leakage, the auditor assigned to Nancy's surgery claim still read her aortic leakage as "mild at most." Furthermore, he attempted to claim numerous "reduction factors" that might have cut Nancy's claim by as much as eighty percent. But her case was simply too solid. After years of fighting—and by then dependent on a walker due to the strain of the surgery—she finally got a reasonable settlement, but it could never make up for her suffering.

Unfortunately, Nancy's situation was pretty typical of the stories we were hearing. Many former fen-phen users were unable to obtain the Trust's free echos—tests that could easily run one thousand dollars out-of-pocket; or they received echos but not their results.

My firm used a company called EchoMotion to perform many of our tests. They were a small company with a very impressive line-up of experienced technicians. But as our remaining days ticked away and the need for echos increased, it was obvious we needed a more efficient plan. We used the Settlement Agreement to hire a full-time team to coordinate echocardiograms according to protocol. We purchased expensive echocardiogram machines and supplies and began the painstaking process of hiring a qualified team of about thirty technicians and assistants. If the Trust was unable or unwilling to provide the free echos, we would take our traveling program directly to the clients.

The echocardiogram test our clients needed was different from what most heart patients would get at their local cardiologists' offices. The Settlement Agreement identified specific items that had to be included, so we tailored our tests accordingly. We arranged for these tests in all fifty states, often processing hundreds, sometimes thousands each week. If the client's echo met our criteria, we then asked for proof that he or she took the drugs. This would usually be a pill bottle, doctor records, or pharmacy records. If they were able to prove they used the drugs, the claims process continued.

Scott Bertram, my co-counsel from Kansas City, and Vance Andrus, trusted former co-counsel and mentor, were in town. The three of us went to dinner, and not surprisingly, the conversation quickly turned to fen-phen. Scott and I bragged that our system was so efficient that potential clients would sign a contract in one room and then have a free echocardiogram performed in the next.

Vance seemed surprised to hear that we were providing expensive tests before we even had proof the clients had taken the required combination. Scott assured him, "Taking the drugs doesn't mean it's a good case. The echo is more exact. We lose about two-thirds due to ..."

"So you go into each case with an expectation that you might reject it?" Vance interrupted. "You're okay wasting your time and money two-thirds of the time?"

Scott answered, "Yeah, it would make sense to do it the other way, but right now there's more money than time, so we have to do it this way."

"How many cases can you take?"

"Until something stops us, there's no limit," I explained. "According to the Trust, they've got to pay a claim or deny it within one hundred-twenty days."

Scott added, "We should get paid at the end of the summer on the cases we submitted to the Trust last month. We'll use that money to advertise for more clients and just continue that cycle until the screening period ends next January."

Vance was skeptical. "It's a risky thing to bank on future settlements to finance existing obligations. In my experience, things don't go that fast. What'll you do if there's a delay?"

"There won't be," I defended. "The Settlement Agreement is strict. This is a binding court order. It's not like we have some punch-drunk claims guy telling us he hopes he can get us the money by Christmas. This is a court order, man."

Scott and I both leaned back a little in our seats to study Vance. I, for one, felt pretty proud of what I thought was an efficient system.

"All I know is what I've lived, and what I've lived tells me this company will find a way to slow things down somehow," he cautioned. "They're not just going to hand over all that money with a smile on their faces."

Vance jotted something on the paper place mat in front of him. He looked up from his notes but kept his thumb over the figure.

"If my math is right, you two already have six thousand cases prepped and ready to go," he mumbled, adjusting his scribbling and shaking his head in disbelief. "I would want a calculator to confirm this—if I could ever find one with enough zeros on it—but this would be almost two hundred million. No ... it would be almost two billion dollars."

"I know it's hard to believe, but that's what we have in our out boxes right now," I replied. "And there are thousands more just coming in."

"I'm worried these guys are going to find a way to put the brakes on all this like Dow did." He was referring to the demise of several hundred breast implant cases and the pending lawsuits that were affected when the company declared bankruptcy. "Maybe it won't be bankruptcy, but they're not just going to sit there and let you take all their money."

After we settled my earlier Round One opt-outs, I took my share and put it all, plus some, into Round Two. I was a risk taker, and

Vance's pessimism was starting to sound like unsolicited advice.

"AHP is much bigger than Dow," I stressed. "They can afford it."

But Vance had the final word. "You put their backs against the wall, and they're going to come after you," he warned. "This is a very powerful corporation, and if it comes down to 'you or them,' it's going to get ugly."

ELEVEN

THE ECHOING OF EARLY WARNINGS

I N EARLY 2002, AHP changed its name to Wyeth. If it was an
attempt to distance itself from the negative publicity, it failed. My
team had been using AHP and Wyeth interchangeably, and while
few seemed to know the name American Home Products, Wyeth was
as famous as its former golden child, fen-phen.

By then, my group had established its rhythm. Teams of echo techs
and site coordinators traveled across the country testing thousands of
former fen-phen users. Doctors were becoming efficient at providing
reports. Low-performing techs improved or went home, and we
experienced fewer and fewer scheduling and travel problems. Our goal
was to keep enlisting new clients throughout the summer. Then, we
could use our momentum in the fall and winter to complete scheduled
testing and evaluate cases before screenings ended and final decisions
were made.

But there was a problem.

Dr. Linda Crouse was a recognized expert on the subject of reading
echocardiograms. Wyeth had employed her as one of its expert readers
years earlier, and now we were counting on her to interpret thousands

of our echocardiograms in order to meet the January 3 deadline.

Jerry Alexander had been by my side during the Lovett trial and eventually opened a branch of his practice in Texas. He knew Dr. Crouse was one of our more trusted and timely readers, which was why he sent her a box of tapes from his Texas office. Omaha, his home base, would follow up by sending her the medical questionnaires containing information related to potential pre-existing heart conditions. Dr. Crouse would need both a tape and medical questionnaire to complete a claim or Green Form. Because the Green Form specifically asked about pre-existing conditions, it was impossible for a doctor to accurately complete the claim form without the patient's questionnaire.

"Kip, are you listening to me?" My hands were shaking and sweaty, making it difficult to hold the phone. Jerry's news left me speechless. "This doctor sent signed Green Forms swearing to patients' medical conditions before my Omaha office even had a chance to send the questionnaires. This looks really, really bad!"

Dr. Crouse had also certified thousands of my own echos. "She's the best, Jerry. Everyone agrees she is the foremost expert." But the Green Form clearly required any doctor to have the questionnaire in hand, so if what Jerry was saying was true, something was terribly wrong.

"Kip, I'm running from this doctor as fast as I can. Will you at least look into it?"

"Man, Jerry. I really don't want to hear about this right now." The thought of thousands of my front-of-the-line claims having to be pulled was depressing. But denial would only delay the inevitable. "But yes, of course I'll look into it."

I began investigating the second I hung up the phone. Dr. Crouse's honesty, integrity, and expertise were being called into question. If I pulled her readings myself, perhaps I could avoid having my character questioned.

Vance's prediction was becoming reality. The claims I had worked so hard to put at the front of the line would lose at least four months. I had most of my cash reserves tied up in these cases, so there was no time to wallow in misery or self-pity.

The Trust also wasted no time. They quickly filed an emergency motion regarding Crouse's work with another law firm.

🏛

The hearing involving Dr. Crouse's work did not directly affect any of my clients' claims, but it was obvious that a ruling against her or her methodologies could affect thousands of Green Forms that she had completed for me. I decided this was too important to watch from the sidelines. I flew to Philadelphia where I spoke with Mike Fishbein, the face of the Nationwide Settlement and Class Counsel, about the matter. I then immediately filed a Motion to Intervene, seeking permission to directly participate in the hearings. Judge Bartle granted a hearing on my motion but swiftly denied my request; I could stay for the proceedings, but I would not be permitted to ask questions or do anything other than observe.

The Lovett trial had been over almost exactly three years. Jerry Alexander and I shared an early cab to the Federal Courthouse in early September of 2002. We made our way through security and into the courtroom on the sixteenth floor. It was large, dwarfing the two teams of lawyers preparing for the hearing to disqualify the Crouse readings. We had been in this courtroom for Round One when Judge Bechtle presided; but he had just retired, and Judge Harvey Bartle was taking over the fen-phen MDL. The hearing began with the usual formalities. Everyone rose as Judge Bartle entered, and the bailiff expressionlessly hollered, "O Ye, O Ye, O Ye. The United States District Court for the Eastern District of Pennsylvania is now in session, The Honorable Harvey J. Bartle, III, Presiding. Draw nigh and ye shall be heard."

Judge Bartle sat, motioning everyone else to do so as well. He allowed the parties to make brief opening statements, and the hearing began with the AHP Settlement Trust vigorously attacking everyone involved with eighty-eight echocardiograms, a pattern that continued for six full days.

One evening, after a long day of listening to evidence, Jerry and I met with Class Counsel members Sol Weiss and Gene Locks for a drink. Sol Weiss had been a friend; he was Class Counsel, like Fishbein, but Sol was much more likable. Years earlier when we brazenly intervened into the MDL, it was Sol who convinced me to settle, get away from the MDL, and save face. Gene was nice enough, but unlike Sol, we were never friendly. He seemed to consider socializing a distasteful duty; he was more of an onlooker.

Two weeks earlier, plaintiffs' attorneys had heard that Wyeth intended to challenge echos based on the location of the test at the time it was performed and on something called "supervision." As Class Counsel, they would know before we would if this was fact or merely rumor. Sol and Gene assured us that doctor supervision, something that was almost unheard of in the world of sonography, would not be an issue with quality echos.

"But," Sol warned, "You should probably know that Wyeth is redefining mitral regurgitation."

"What do you mean redefining?" Jerry asked. He looked at me, one eyebrow cocked high on his forehead. He and I had shared our own suspicions about the very subject.

"Redefining," Sol repeated. "They're rewriting the definition, you know, so that fewer people will qualify." The way the settlement was originally written, maximum leakage was used to determine benefits. Sol explained that the way Wyeth was redefining it, something closer to average would be used instead.

"They're meddling," Sol added. "They've agreed to 'interpret' the settlement in their favor."

"How can they do that?" I asked.

THE ECHOING OF EARLY WARNINGS

"How can you complain?" Gene leaned forward, placing his large elbows on the table and gesturing palms up toward me. "You've got thousands of cases, Kip. Napoli and Bern have been caught being pigs. You want to go get behind them in line to complain to the judge?" Gene was referring to Paul Napoli and Marc Bern, two New York lawyers who got thrown under the bus by a disgruntled echo tech. And while the echo technician was eventually discredited, the charges still led to hearings that led to a decision that most of their challenged cases had been medically unreasonable. None of us wanted to be in their shoes.

At the same time, once the Settlement Agreement was finalized, it should have been completely inappropriate for Wyeth or anyone else to tinker. Class Counsel and the Trust were allowing it to happen. The new interpretations would completely wipe out legitimate cases.

Based on the original agreement, our sonographers identified what they thought were the maximum jets, highlighted them, and then traced and measured them. They were told there would be random audits, so they were as meticulous as possible with their measurements. The files were then given to a cardiologist for their expert input, and then our attorneys sent the entire package to the Trust, where we assumed their doctors would double check all measurements. And while we knew they would sometimes disagree with our interpretations, we welcomed the scrutiny, which would help guide us in our efforts to continue testing our clients.

We simply followed what we were told were the rules. Eighty thousand of our clients had already received echos according to these criteria. Now, three-quarters of the way through the screening period, they were changing the rules.

When the interpretation of maximum became more like average, this made sonographers' jobs more complex and broadened the potential for disagreement and error. Anyone who has ever seen a baby's sonogram understands that the images are nearly indecipherable to most people, and even to the trained eye, they are still sometimes difficult to interpret. So expecting a cardiologist or sonographer to identify an exact mathematical average on a fuzzy three-dimensional image of rapidly moving fluid, when they are dealing with 19.999% versus 20.001%, was unrealistic.

And perhaps the most unfathomable part of the equation was the end result. A claimant with 19.999% leakage would receive nothing, whereas a person with 20.001% could be eligible for hundreds of thousands of dollars in damages.

When we learned the Trust was questioning our experts' interpretations, we asked them to make their own measurements, but they refused. We gave the Trust the sonographer's notes and printouts of the measurements along with electronic copies of the original echocardiogram tapes and disks, so they had everything our experts had for comparison. If they read the echos themselves, they would prove us right in many cases, which would lead to money damages for the clients. Instead, by redefining the agreement and by invalidating tests that they considered improperly supervised, Wyeth and the Trust could avoid the Trust running out of money or Wyeth going bankrupt.

In the recent hearings, notes were being passed, conversations whispered and documents quietly discussed as the three—Wyeth, Class Counsel and the Trust—worked as one right under the judge's nose. They united to break away any footing the claimants and their doctors and lawyers might have built for themselves. Savvy attorneys know how to communicate in court without it becoming part of the official record. This gang's silent actions spoke volumes about misplaced loyalties—the duplicitous lawyering of those who should have been advocating for the claimants.

I had suspected some sort of collusion all along, but what I saw, supported by Sol and Gene's story, painted a picture of Class Counsel and the Trust flaunting their love affair with Wyeth in plain sight. Despite my revulsion, I was also partly relieved. To hear them say that

Wyeth wanted to redefine essential terms meant that the Settlement Agreement was the problem and not our interpretation of it. Still, it also meant many clients' claims were in trouble.

I had always expected Wyeth to play hardball; after all, it was their pockets I was trying to empty. But once the Trust was established, Wyeth should not have been allowed that much influence. The Trust was established to decide who got paid according to settlement instructions. It was not an adversarial task, nor should it have been a partnership. If a client's claim was to be denied, that was the Trust's business, not Wyeth's. Class Counsel, unfortunately, did not see it that way.

I sat at the back of the courtroom for one of Judge Bartle's monthly status conferences not long after the Crouse hearings. I always took notes and had been doing so when I ran out of paper. I stood to get my briefcase, which was just a step away. But, as I reached, I was shocked to hear my name called from the front of the courtroom. I turned to see Mike Fishbein, holding a small stack of papers, calling me to the podium. He must have thought I was leaving and wanted to stop me. The courtroom fell silent and all eyes were on me. The papers were a memo I had written many years previously. Fishbein said that I, as a leader in fen-phen, was scamming the system. I was caught off guard. Up to that point, the two of us had disagreed, but now he was openly attacking me. I glanced at the memo and acknowledged that I wrote it. "I stand by every word."

"I couldn't have said it better myself," Fish bellowed red-faced.

The memo was my attempt to explain to co-counsel that they were over-valuing some of their cases. Some of our experts had used the criteria from the Nationwide Settlement to render opinions about the heart health of about two hundred clients, but other experts had used traditional and more stringent criteria. I explained that the lawyers whose experts used the Nationwide Settlement criteria had unrealistically high return expectations for their clients because its definition of moderate mitral leakage was not employed in the real world. The memo went on to say that mitral valve cases that were moderate, according to the Matrix definition of moderate, were now only going to be considered mild in the opt-out settlement. Fishbein, or Fish, as we liked to call him, used that portion of the memo to tell Judge Bartle, in open court, that I was scamming the system. But, because we had excluded all but three of our clients from the Nationwide Settlement before the memo was written, the exact opposite was actually true.

Despite Fish's dramatic outburst and attempt to criminalize the memo, Judge Bartle seemed unimpressed and disinterested. But Fish had opened my eyes. He, or someone pulling his strings, had decided I was a threat. Vance had warned me that, if it came down to them or me, Wyeth would come after me. Crouse had been the first. She cut corners and was humiliated. Her shortcuts had made everyone else's actions questionable. Class Counsel was helping the Trust fight claimants and their doctors. We were at the precipice of a modern day witch hunt, and by the grace of God, I had just narrowly escaped the gallows—but only narrowly.

Tucked deep within the "Claims Administration" section of the four-inch thick Settlement Agreement was the statement that all echocardiograms were to be "conducted under the supervision of, and read and interpreted by, a board-certified cardiologist or board-certified cardiothoracic surgeon with level two training in echocardiography, as specified in the 'Recommendations of the American Society of Echocardiography Committee on Physician Training in Echocardiography.'"

THE ECHOING OF EARLY WARNINGS

The Trust began asserting, late in the game, that "supervised" meant that the doctor was physically present and watching during the echocardiogram. Such supervision was practically unheard of outside of fen-phen. Technicians undergo rigorous training and certification, and most cardiologists' time is simply too valuable for this to be realistic. No one would have deliberately ignored the supervision language in the Settlement Agreement. The supervision sentence made up just one line out of many thousands. No one noticed it, nor did the circumstances merit looking for such a thing. We conducted our echos with experienced echo techs in the manner in which they were done in the real world of medicine—without a doctor hovering.

One of the first motions the Trust filed asserting its supervision defense was the "EchoMotion Motion." More specifically, it was the "Motion to Disqualify All EchoMotion Echocardiograms from Supporting Claims for Benefits." Behind the scenes, everyone agreed that quality echos were the goal. But publicly there was talk of massive disqualification of unsupervised echos. We had become extremely vulnerable. Ironically, it appeared most of the echos done through my firm's efforts were superior to the ones the Trust had performed. There were hundreds of so-called "unsupervised" echos that identified life-threatening problems—and not just those related to fen-phen usage.

🏛

Jim Sartor took fen-phen and then, several years later, he took me up on my offer of a free echo at a Ramada Inn. Our screening found that he had severe aortic leakage, but echo techs are not doctors and are not permitted to diagnose problems. The tech was concerned Jim was a walking time bomb and sent him to a cardiologist right away.

Doctors told Jim he needed surgery, but he could not afford to take off work or pay the up-front costs; so I loaned him the money. During the procedure, doctors found that Jim had an aortic dissection or tear in the aorta. This was the same heart condition that had apparently killed actor John Ritter. Ritter was wealthy and had all the resources needed to detect the congenital defect in his aorta. The actor made sure his doctors knew his family's heart history, and he had even had a full body scan two years earlier. Yet he died suddenly at age fifty-four after being misdiagnosed with a heart attack. Was it luck that Jim's hotel echo found for him what John Ritter's multiple doctor and hospital visits missed, even after the actor became ill?

But the Trust wanted to cheapen our echos, like Jim's, not because they found issue with the quality, but because they were performed in hotels.

Furthermore, the Trust paid over a thousand dollars for each echo it obtained. We did roughly a hundred thousand of them when it appeared they were unable or unwilling to keep up with the demand, saving the Trust a hundred million dollars, an argument I thought might make some headway with Wayne and Jerry.

"That will get you nowhere," Wayne's voice crackled over the speakerphone. "We made the same point. The Trust says you can't prove they couldn't provide sufficient echos to everyone because you didn't request them for everyone."

"Yeah, and now that the screening period is over, they claim they would have handled them fine if all your clients had come to them," Jerry added.

Wayne continued, "They also say they could have gotten permission to extend the screening period if needed; they've done it twice already. In other words, it was nice of you to try to help them, but your echos still weren't supervised."

"Then what about proving that the Trust echos were done the same as ours? Several of our doctors also worked for the Trust. They say there's no difference." The silence on the other end of the line encouraged me. I hoped, at least, that this argument could gain some traction.

Jerry replied, "It certainly makes the lack of supervision look innocent and not diabolical if the Trust made the same mistake everyone else did."

Encouraged by Jerry's response, I added, "I'm going to try to identify clients who had unsupervised echos done through the screening program." I added, "How can the Trust invalidate all the echos they already performed for nearly two hundred thousand people? They already made thousands of payments, and it wasn't an issue then. We're talking two billion dollars in Matrix payments and another couple hundred million in echo costs."

"Scheff doesn't care," Wayne responded.

Richard Scheff was a former U.S. Prosecutor who famously toppled corrupt Philadelphia judges. Now he worked for the Settlement Trust as Special Counsel. Rumor had it that he despised plaintiffs' attorneys. "Those payments were not made on his watch, and most of the echos were conducted before he came on board. All he cares about is making sure unsupervised echos aren't paid or even processed while he is in charge."

"All unsupervised echos are disqualified. That's what he says. No exceptions," Jerry added.

"He's out for blood," Wayne replied, "and if he has to shed a little of his own to make you bleed out, he'll do it."

They attacked us; now it was our turn to attack them. We used the method we knew best—the courts. We served the Trust with formal discovery requests, demanding that they provide documents concerning communications with screening program doctors and cardiac sonographers. After much negotiating, they complied. The Green Form did not mention supervision, and the doctors did not receive the Settlement Agreement, so there was no way they could have known about supervision any more than our doctors or sonographers could have.

Then plaintiffs' lawyers were collectively given ninety minutes in which they could depose the Trust's Executive Director, Robert Mitchell. I took the lead on this. The deposition was set for November 14, 2002, in Philadelphia with twenty-seven lawyers observing. Ninety minutes would be rushing it, but I was convinced I could do it if the witness cooperated.

Every plaintiff's lawyer with clients who filed Green Forms was interested in the Trust's position on supervision. Those who thought they conducted properly supervised echos were eager to see if theirs met the criteria. Those with arguably unsupervised or "loosely-supervised" echos wanted theirs compared to the Trust's. We were determined to demonstrate that the location of the test was not important, that the Trust did not supervise its own echocardiograms, that the Trust had been unconcerned with supervision when paying earlier claims, and that plaintiffs' lawyers' echos were just as good as those the Trust had performed.

I asked Dr. Mitchell to verify that the Trust never asked where echos were performed in previously paid claims, despite having shelled out almost a billion dollars. He confirmed saying, "The location of where the echos were done doesn't make any difference."

I even suggested that, if a doctor's office versus the back of a pickup truck was in question, "I mean has the Trust ever cared where the echos are done?"

"No," he verified.

"Has Wyeth, to your knowledge?" I asked.

"Not as long as—" Mitchell hesitated, glancing toward the Trust's lawyers and Fishbein, then finally gave the answer we sought, "No."

Mitchell agreed that the Trust never specifically informed screening program doctors about the need to supervise echocardiograms. He also agreed that an echocardiogram could be acceptable even if the doctor was unaware how the echo was acquired and knew nothing about the technician's identity or qualifications. Furthermore, the Trust failed to ask if there was supervision of echos before paying almost a billion dollars.

The Mitchell deposition was widely read, so we hoped the Trust would drop the supervision issues to save its own echos. But battle lines had already been drawn, and any collateral damage was just the cost of winning the war. If it took sacrificing its own clients and their echos to justify disqualifying our echos, then so be it.

Vance Andrus' earlier warning echoed in my mind ... *"You put their backs against the wall, and they're going to come after you, and it's going to get ugly."*

TWELVE

NUCLEAR WAR

JANUARY 3, 2003 brought a close to the screening period. Weeks later Vance Andrus sat across from me at a small cocktail table in the bar of the Ritz Carlton Hotel in Philadelphia.

"I'm not even sure I can keep the firm afloat until this is over," I admitted. I was exhausted from trying to hold my crumbling marriage together. Dana and I had begun fighting soon after getting married. That, and my battles with the Trust and bill collectors, left me feeling completely overwhelmed.

"You didn't hold back a chunk of money to use in case things didn't work out like you planned?" Vance asked.

"Didn't think I'd need it. I just kept putting in more money, close to one hundred-twenty percent of what I made on Round One," I told him.

"I guess I'm not surprised. I've watched you making co-counsel deals and spending money like there was no end to your supply."

"Guess I didn't count on them dragging this out. Claims processing has all but stopped." I threw back the last of my drink and ordered another. At six bucks a shot, it would be my last until I got back to the cheap bottle in my room.

"I'm surprised you didn't run into this problem sooner," he said, not wanting to use the words *I told you so.* It was just one of the reasons I respected him. He was wise, but he wasn't a wise ass. He had tried to warn Scott Bertram and me to hold back some money from Round One, but we had been too sure of ourselves to listen.

"Here's the thing, Vance," I started. "The screening period is over, and with the echos done, the major financial hemorrhaging is over. But we still have to pay to have all these tapes read and processed, and that costs money."

Vance shook his head and smiled. "Man, Kip. You're a victim of your own success. You're the Pied Piper of attorneys. You stand up at one of these seminars, and lawyers come from all over the place and throw their cases at your feet. They treat you like a big shot, follow you around and ask you questions, and they even eavesdrop when you talk to other people. You've got the thousands of cases you wanted; now what're you gonna do with 'em all?"

"My only problem is the Trust," I excused. "I'd never need to borrow a penny the rest of my life if the Trust met their four-month timetable on just a handful of our cases."

Vance interrupted, "Man, don't you know? The Trust can't even open its daily mail within four months of receiving it."

We laughed at the joke, but it did not solve my problems. "And they don't show any signs of ever getting caught up. They're bleeding me. I pay the echo techs, I pay the doctors and I pay employees and records services. It would be nice if someone would pay me for a change."

"A plaintiff's lawyer who is case rich and cash poor. It's not a new phenomenon." Vance stirred his drink and added, "What happens when the Trust is broke? You can't assume these claims will all be paid. It's time you consider what happens when the Trust runs out of money."

Vance did not hear my call for help. Perhaps he would respond to a more direct approach. "I have spoken to a couple bankers, and my credit lines with Merrill Lynch and Themis Capital are tapped out. No one wants to—or is willing to—loan me more money until there's some action. Of course, that doesn't help me because if there was action, I wouldn't need to borrow money. I don't know where else to turn, Vance, except perhaps a fellow lawyer like you who might recognize the value of these cases."

Vance stared down at his drink without changing his expression. He had been expecting my request. He picked up the empty glass, rattled the ice, and set it down a few inches further in toward the middle of the table. He was done drinking for the night.

"I'm not making any promises," he said, "But I have some lawyer friends who might be willing to put together a pot of money to help you through the lean times. Maybe. *Maybe not*. I'll see if there's any interest in helping you with this thing. No promises."

"Vance, I'm telling you, I'll pay them—"

"We're not talking about some cozy little loan that you might get from a bank," he interrupted. "The lawyers I'm talking about are gamblers, adventurers—not bankers. They're all lawyers who have been where you've been. They were young once, too. They'll want a piece of the action if they are going to put up the money to see this thing through."

He was proposing a partnership. After all my hard work and my own investment, they would want a cut just like they had been on board the whole time. There was no other option. The longer I waited, the more desperate I would become.

"I got it," I assured him. "I understand your guys need to see a possible big bang for their buck."

That "bang" came to be known as the Andrus Agreement and came at a cost of seven and a half percent of my fen-phen fees. In return, Vance would come on as a consultant, and there were times his advice was at least as valuable as his money.

By the end of the screening period, on January 3, 2003, my law firm arranged and paid for about one hundred thousand echocardiograms. Some claims were processed during that period, too, but our main focus had been screening as many clients as possible. Rather than feeling relief at the long-anticipated end of the screening period, we then began a new race: we had four months to determine how to proceed with the claims that remained.

At one point, we had hired about twenty paralegals and six lawyers, but with so many clients, we still had to call on outside help. Much of the work was farmed out to experienced and capable satellite law firms throughout the country who performed the same services for our mutual clients as my own lawyers but on a smaller scale. New echo testing stopped when the screening period ended, and at that point, our remaining cases were all in varying stages of completeness. We now had less than four months to process everyone. This basically consisted of five steps:

1) The echo tape, along with a corresponding questionnaire, had to be copied and sent to a board certified cardiologist;

2) He or she prepared a separate written report on each echo;

3) Our lawyers analyzed the doctors' reports;

4) These same lawyers then decided if the client met the criteria for acceptance as a viable case;

5) The client and referring attorney were then notified of our recommendation, or, if they qualified as both opt-ins and opt-outs, they worked with an attorney to make the best choice for themselves.

At step four, everyone was either rejected or accepted. About ninety percent of our original one hundred thousand clients were rejected for various reasons but mostly because they were too healthy or could not prove they had used fen-phen.

About two months before the May 3 opt-out deadline, someone discovered that several paralegals had inadvertently rejected a sizable number of cases for lacking the required leakage level. They had not realized that some of the potential clients had already had their hearts repaired before coming to us. Their new echocardiograms showed no leakage, but the individuals were still eligible for a claim based on the fact they had sought earlier medical care. In their files, the doctors' interpretations indicated "normal readings." Because notes about the valve repair or replacement were in a separate location, many of these clients were unduly rejected.

These were some of the most valuable potential claims to come across our desks. Had the mistakes not been caught when they were, we could have jeopardized the clients' ability to claim damages. Every rejected file had to be re-reviewed.

At that point, it was hard to trust anyone to do the job, and hiring someone this late in the game was out of the question. Robert would have been perfect; if he had been there, the paralegals would have been properly trained to identify the surgery cases.

Then Stan Hudson became available. I had hired Stan, an experienced registered pharmacist and a board certified trial lawyer, two years earlier to take care of other, more challenging cases. He had tackled everything with superb attention to detail. Because Round Two of fen-phen had been mostly paper pushing up to this point, I had shielded him from it; he was overqualified. But he was the closest thing to a "Robert" I had. This was just the type of job a detail guy would nail.

Thanks to Stan, we finally got the surgery cases ironed out—just in time for the deadline. The "reject" files were put aside, and we continued to focus on what remained of the unfortunate ten percent we accepted—unfortunate because they had been determined to have a genuine health concern. Clients we accepted had to meet certain minimum requirements. They had to be at least "FDA Positive," which meant, at minimum, mild aortic or moderate mitral leakage as defined by the Settlement Agreement.

We analyzed each one to see if it appeared that the client would do better on the Matrix (which meant he or she made a claim for settlement benefits), or as an opt-out (meaning he or she decided to forego the class action settlement and would instead file a lawsuit in court). There were pros and cons to each option. The Matrix would pay some clients, mainly those with mitral leakage, hundreds of thousands of dollars, and they did not have to prove the drugs caused injury, that they were sick, or that they had any symptoms. They only needed an abnormal echo and to fit onto the chart. On the whole, this option was best for those with mitral valve leakage.

On the other hand, the Matrix was not a good option for clients with aortic damage because they would receive just up to six thousand dollars. At the same time, aortic damage was the type directly linked to fen-phen usage, and it would be easier to prove in court—as we had with Debbie Lovett. Opting out was often the better choice for these clients.

Pre-lawsuit preparation for opt-out claims was tedious. Most clients had no idea how much work they would have to do and how much their private lives would be interrupted and exposed. They would be expected to miss some work, and their families and friends would be asked to make sacrifices. The questions the defense team would pose in depositions were often humiliating, personal, and totally unnecessary, including questions about ex-spouses, mental health, and even sexual and social habits. Almost nothing was off limits because everything could somehow lead to additional evidence.

Wyeth's lawyers knew these questions were irritating and intrusive, and they used them to their advantage. About forty percent of our potential opt-out clients caved in under the pressure when they heard about the toxic Wyeth depositions. Many others agreed to maintain their lawsuits but refused to go to trial if they could not settle.

In the beginning, tens of thousands hired me hoping for

easy money, but there had been nothing easy about the road from echocardiogram to payday.

🏛

Wyeth refused to discuss the settlement of any opt-out cases until after the May 3, 2003 claims deadline. The company line up to that point had been that its lawyers were prepared to try every case. Any other approach could have encouraged a massive flood of opt-outs from those hoping to receive more than six thousand dollars. Then, in early June, just weeks after the opt-out deadline, Wyeth said they were ready to talk settlement. Fifty or so plaintiffs' attorneys met in Dallas for the occasion just days later.

Dicky Scruggs, Ed Blizzard, and I were elected to negotiate on behalf of all plaintiffs' attorneys. What we hoped to achieve was a fair, peaceful, non-combative resolution of tens of thousands of cases. The panel in attendance on Wyeth's behalf was impressive and included Peter Zimroth from the New York office of Arnold and Porter.

Ed Blizzard formally presented most of our arguments, and Ellen Reisman and Peter Zimroth tag teamed on Wyeth's behalf. No one discussed money at first, but all settlement meetings must go there eventually. When Blizzard proposed twelve billion dollars to settle everything, it was as though a massive steam engine traveling at top speed had suddenly derailed itself. Zimroth fumed that our demand was so far out in the stratosphere that they would not even bother to make a response. The meeting ended abruptly, giving us little to report back to the eager plaintiffs' attorneys who had sent us.

Another settlement meeting in New York weeks later also went nowhere.

It appeared to many that the meetings had been staged so that the defense team could tell Wyeth that it tried to settle twice, but "the greedy lawyers were too greedy." This would allow Arnold and Porter to continue launching aggressive and expensive attacks while sticking Wyeth with the legal bill.

Quite a few of the attorneys who represented plaintiffs in Round Two only got involved because they thought it would be easy. Most had no intention of going to court, and even fewer were willing to battle the barrage of threats and motions. One after another gave up, and many of the attorneys who remained were battered and weak—easy targets for the opposition.

A conference call with Wayne and Jerry was not what I wanted or needed. But there was work to be done, and the two of them were poised on both sides of the fight. Apparently my name had received top billing at a recent meeting in Philadelphia.

"They all give you their best, by the way," Wayne joked.

"Seriously, Kip," Jerry cut to the chase, "they specifically used the word 'fraud' several times, and they said there needs to be some 'bloodletting'—also their word."

"In fact," Wayne added, "Ellen Reisman specifically mentioned your name when she said they'd been naïve to think you guys would be reasonable."

"They say they are getting pounded with calls from opt-out lawyers desperate to settle their cases at any price," Jerry reported. I had hoped the plaintiffs' lawyers would at least act like they intended to try their cases rather than show their vulnerability by hitting up Wyeth for early low-ball settlements.

Lawyers had been calling our office, too, wanting to unload their cases onto us when their requests for early settlements were denied or ignored.

"That could be," I said, "but some of us like to fight. Wyeth warned it would be a scorched earth, no-holds-barred brawl, but we opted cases out anyway." Then I added, "By the way, you don't think I haven't figured out that Wyeth is using you to get to me? Their mouths to my ears—by way of you, of course. But that works both ways. You tell them I'm just getting warmed up."

🏛

Fifteen boxes stood in the doorway when I arrived at the office not long after. They were full of forms Wayne had warned me to expect. Redonda had set a sample where I would be sure to see it. I stood, briefcase in hand, and began reading. They were called Medical Practice Questionnaires, eighteen pages printed on cover stock, and full of sections typed in all caps and angry, bold type. Doctors were being asked to swear under "penalty of perjury" to the claimant's condition and to provide information as to their methodologies. It was a far cry from what the doctors originally agreed to do: look at a tape and claimant's questionnaire and complete a Green Form. Now, they were being told to swear to numerous additional facts they had not been asked to pay attention to before, and if someone decided they were wrong, the stakes were perjury.

This had to be Scheff's handiwork, and he had already sued Linda Crouse, attacking her methodology. The entire thing had an eerily threatening tone, and I feared doctors would refuse. Wayne had explained it was all part of Scheff's Claims Integrity Program. "He's convinced Judge Bartle will applaud his efforts to weed out fraud. In his opinion, this shouldn't be too much to ask," he had said. "I don't think Scheff is going to want to bargain much when lawyers with lots of claims start whining about how time-consuming it's going to be."

Doctors would have every right to charge by the hour to complete the lengthy forms. The Trust knew it; they were counting on it. Those of us who remained active in the litigation were becoming financially anemic. *This is what bloodletting feels like*, I thought to myself. I could struggle and make things worse, or I could give them what they wanted and try to recuperate afterward.

I envied Robert, my former partner, sitting in college classes learning the finer points of history from professors close to his own age alongside pretty co-eds half his age.

THIRTEEN

FIGHTING ON MULTIPLE FRONTS

A S A PART of the original Nationwide Settlement, Wyeth gave up most of its statute of limitations defenses and most claimants gave up their ability to seek punitive damages. The only people who could still sue for punitive damages were claimants with PPH and those who opted out of the Nationwide Settlement by March 30, 2000.

In 1999, a jury had awarded one hundred-fifty million dollars to five fen-phen plaintiffs for compensatory damages alone, pressuring Wyeth to settle the rest of that attorney's remaining cases. And in the fall of 2003, just a few counties away, a Jackson, Mississippi judge agreed to set my Mary Jones vs. Wyeth case for trial.

Mary Jones's case was an unusual one. She had been excluded from a settlement with her previous attorney, and her file languished for well over a year until it came to me. It was a solid punitive damage case when few remained, and it was in Mississippi, a state in which Wyeth had a poor track record. I felt like I had found a rare masterpiece at a garage sale. This was my best remaining chance to prove gross negligence before a jury as we had done in Debbie Lovett's case, but the jury would be even more sympathetic in Mississippi. Its placement at the beginning of a long trail of non-punitive cases could help establish a higher value, or if we were unsuccessful, a lower one.

In the summer of 2003, two well-known fen-phen witnesses looked like they could make the powerful impression we needed. And, much to my surprise, both responded favorably to my initial requests. Pam Ruff was an echo tech in Fargo, North Dakota. Many people credit her with first identifying the presence of unusual heart valve leakage in otherwise healthy young women who had taken fen-phen. The doctors had failed to take her seriously, but after heart valve cases continued to amass at their small hospital, one eventually agreed to contact the Mayo Clinic. As it turned out, the Mayo Clinic was already working on a study about similar issues, so the Fargo patients were included. The Mayo Clinic then contacted Wyeth with their fifteen new valve cases, including Ruff's.

Initially, the Mayo Clinic cases were coded at the drug company as involving heart valves. Then, Wyeth decided that events labeled as heart valve problems could be damaging if reported in association with fen-phen. A Wyeth employee, Amy Myers, changed the coding to one of the other minor symptoms the patient had reported, like headaches or constipation. Yet Wyeth still defended their inability to spot trouble because of the sheer numbers of people taking the drugs and the natural presence of valve disease in the general public. Having an echo tech from Fargo explain how it had jumped right out at her would undermine Wyeth's excuses.

It was surprising to hear that no one had contacted Ms. Ruff in the years since her discovery, and I was pleased she agreed to speak to me. I eagerly designated her as a witness, and as is procedure, informed the defense team. Then, just as suddenly as she agreed to speak, she stopped speaking altogether. Phone call after phone call went unanswered. I never heard from her again, and I never learned why.

I still had one remaining hope. Dr. Leo Lutwak was one of the

FDA medical officers charged with monitoring the safety of new and recently approved prescription medicines. During the Lovett trial, we had heard he wanted to talk. We got permission from Judge Wallace to send the equivalent of a subpoena to the FDA so that we could depose him in Washington, but his federal employer steadfastly refused. His absence from Lovett had not made a difference, but now, with Ruff suddenly uncooperative, we wanted him more than ever.

In the summer of 2003, retired from the FDA, Dr. Lutwak was finally free to speak to me. Not only was he cooperative, he was very eager. This witness was not about to be spooked. We scheduled his deposition for late summer, but it was postponed several times due to his ailing health. He had macular degeneration and also suffered from severe emphysema. In mid-fall, he stabilized enough to meet with us.

When we arrived at the deposition location, Peter Bleakley was waiting in the seat normally reserved for the questioning attorney. Bleakley was a top Arnold and Porter attorney. Along with his partner Peter Grossi, he won Wyeth's only initial opt-out victory to date. Bleakley and Grossi commanded more respect than the rest of their firm combined, so Bleakley's presence confirmed Dr. Lutwak's importance.

I recognized everyone in the room except two passive, expressionless dark suits. Unlike the others, who had legal pads and pens and milled about socially, these two appeared to have very little to do but observe. I greeted them both with a smile and a handshake, and they each handed me a business card. It was only later that I glanced at their cards: "Drake Cutine, Esq., United States Department of Justice, Office of Consumer Litigation" and "Candace K. Ambrose, Esq., U.S. Food and Drug Administration." This should have raised concern, but I was so focused on the work ahead that I paid little attention.

Then the trademark white hair caught my eye. It was whiter than in the doctor's recent picture, quite disheveled and there was less of it, but he still had the goatee-style beard and moustache giving him the appearance of the quintessential scientist. Dr. Lutwak was quite a colorful character amongst all the stiff suits and shiny shoes. I liked the man tremendously.

Large glasses covered much of his small face, and the thick lenses exaggerated his sickly eyes. His clothes hung off his skeletal body like a man who had once weighed twice as much; if not for his red suspenders, his pants would surely have been six inches too big for his deteriorating waistline. He was burdened by an irritating cough, which once started, quickly drained him of any energy. He seemed to be fading before our eyes.

The doctor's testimony would, at times, sound like the script for a spy movie. He was a compassionate and honest scientist who dedicated his career to protecting and saving lives. But, during his tenure, philosophies shifted at the FDA; the interests of the pharmaceutical companies began taking precedence over consumer safety. Dr. Lutwak had voiced his concern that Pondimin was dangerous, and he spoke out firmly against Redux in an attempt to "prevent this lethal agent from being unleashed." But his superiors at the FDA shut him out, determined to ignore the red flags.

After reaching disappointing dead ends, Dr. Lutwak then turned his attention to getting warnings and restrictions on the drug's label. Instead of being celebrated for his concern for consumer safety, Dr. Lutwak was demoted, moved into positions he considered irrelevant within the agency, and eventually put out to pasture.

Author Alicia Mundy had written about Dr. Lutwak in her book *Dispensing with the Truth.* The tragic protagonist in her story was Mary Linnen. Mary had taken fen-phen for twenty-three days to lose weight for her wedding, but her doctor stopped the meds when the young bride-to-be complained of shortness of breath. She was later diagnosed with primary pulmonary hypertension after experiencing loss of breath, dizziness, extreme tiredness, and limb swelling. After her fiancé, Tom, carried her up the stairs one night, she said that something wrong; her breathing was getting worse. Mary was soon pronounced dead. She and Tom never married.

Mary's sister contacted Dr. Lutwak after reading about him in Mundy's book, explaining that her sister's death had devastated her family. He cried all night after that call.

In his deposition, Dr. Lutwak described how the FDA lost its power to the big drug companies and how he had felt stifled and unable to do his job. His descriptions of real victims were a reminder that these were people, not files, cases, or dollar signs. They were complex, meaningful, flesh-and-blood lives.

Just because he was old and sick did not mean he was any less sharp. He was still a top scientist, with his wits fully intact. As Bleakley questioned him, Dr. Lutwak cleverly inserted bits of testimony into his answers that he hoped would one day come back and haunt Wyeth. He believed they had not been punished enough, and he was determined to see them pay for the damage they had caused. Yet, despite his determination, he appeared to become weaker as the hours passed. The simple task of talking became a chore; he was fragile and required frequent breaks.

Dana had come to the deposition, even though we were separated. Despite our growing differences, we had reconciled at least our friendship, with an occasional romantic side trip, and I needed the friendly, supportive company. She had been a paralegal prior to our marriage, so I knew she could also help me with the deposition. I had no idea Dr. Lutwak would take to her like he did. Despite his near blindness, he could see she was beautiful, and she and the doctor took smoke breaks together. Wyeth's attorneys, annoyed at the delays, insisted Dana was a spy.

After two days, we took a three-week break. When we returned, Bleakley came prepared with massive reproductions of key documents. The doctor's vision had been so bad that, prior to the break, he had been unable to see the smaller versions, so the defense team thought the blow-ups would elicit more cooperation. But nothing helped; Dr. Lutwak's vision was deteriorating very quickly. Bleakley, normally calm and cool, was clearly frustrated. There's an expression in law: never abuse Grandma (or in the doctor's case, Grandpa). Bleakley was forced to accept the elder gentleman's word.

After four days of deposition, Dr. Lutwak had become so frail that we finally quit. He had so much more he wanted to say, and we still had unanswered questions. But he was falling apart, and we had what we came for: the video-taped testimony of a courageous former FDA official criticizing the drug company in the strongest possible words. His gravelly voice, thick with disease, idled over certain words as though they deserved a greater share of the oxygen that pumped from the tank by his side. "Whoever, whether an individual or group of individuals, was responsible for the whole fenfluramine situation, it's as reprehensible and criminal as the individuals who drove planes into the World Trade Center and bombed the Pentagon. I think that if we ever get a final accounting, we will find that these individuals were responsible for more deaths, more lasting damage. And the only way anything can be done to prevent this from happening again is by exposing it."

Dr. Lutwak had provided some of the most inflammatory and credible testimony in fen-phen. Wyeth knew its potential for damage, so they promptly settled Mary Jones's case and several other initial opt-out cases. This completely neutralized Dr. Lutwak's damning testimony, which could not be used in non-punitive cases—all that remained following the settlements.

Dr. Leo Lutwak lived another three years, surpassing everyone's expectations—perhaps even his own. He was a scientist, concerned physician, and star witness. His death on February 23, 2006, at the age of 78, was a great loss to humanity.

The monthly status conference in Judge Bartle's court in September 2003 was the first I had missed in over a year. Instead, I had been in Maryland working on the Mary Jones case that had been set for trial the following month. Jerry called from Philly to tell me what I had missed. I was aboard the train, about halfway there myself, and needed help passing time.

"The day was a disaster," he exclaimed. "It was horrible. So many bad things happened that I don't even know where to begin. Among other things, Judge Bartle literally said, 'who cares what Rob Mitchell testified to?' Something about an echo in the back of a pickup truck?"

Mitchell was the Trust's lawyer and executive director who had earlier said the location where an echocardiogram was performed was irrelevant. We had hoped to use Mitchell's testimony in the supervision hearing, and Bartle had apparently suggested we would be wasting our time.

Jerry continued, "Fishbein described the unique 'constellation' of facts that invalidate an echo, and it sounded like a legitimate summary of the way echos are usually done."

I could hear him on the other end of the phone shuffling papers, probably skimming his stack of notes. "Let's see what else was of importance ..." There was a tinge of excitement, and then, "Oh yeah, Scheff was there." Despite his omnipresence, none of us had actually seen Richard Scheff, a huge, frightening, god-like figure staring down from some untouchable place. "He seems to think he's 'at one' with Bartle—calm, cool, collected—the rest of us sweating bullets."

"See what happens when I'm absent for just one hearing?" I joked.

Then his tone tightened. "Oh. I had a conversation with Sol Weiss after the hearing." Jerry switched to the tone of voice reserved for bad news. "I don't know what to make of it, and consider the source, but Sol went out of his way to say that 'they,' and I don't know who 'they' are, but according to him, 'they're' going after you, Kip, and he specifically mentioned you by name. This sounds like Scheff. He's got a gigantic operating budget and the sympathy of a federal judge who's already apprehensive."

"Anything else?" I asked, afraid of the answer.

"That's it, man, and to tell you the truth," Jerry added, "Sol kind of caught me off-guard. He was being so direct—too direct, like he was giving me a message to give to you. Man, Kip, I thought Sol was some kind of friend of yours."

He was—or at least had been—as had Jerry and Wayne. "People change," I offered, trying to ignore the uneasiness that had begun stirring in my stomach.

"And of course, Fishbein is salivating at the idea of seeing some of his colleagues indicted for scamming the system. Kip, I'm hearing a lot of things that are just really, really scary."

I found an excuse to hang up, but the truth was that Jerry's motives were becoming hazy. The threat probably was not his, but he delivered it like a kid who had been coached by some bigger kid—a bully with an agenda. It was getting harder to separate the message from the messenger.

Then came the weekend of my parents' anniversary celebration. Wayne called Friday to tell me I was the target of a Civil RICO investigation. Jerry's warning that "they" were coming after me appeared true. I had to keep that secret to myself the rest of the weekend, which made it impossible for me to relax and enjoy the festivities. I struggled with whether or not I should continue to fight or just swim out into the ocean and end the misery. But fight what? "They" were as much a mystery as the thing they were accusing me of doing wrong. But, based on the Dr. Crouse situation and the threats I had heard over and over again, it was serious.

A few days later, Wayne emailed me: "I was told this morning that you are a day or two away from being served with a Civil RICO complaint. I believe Sol is the source of this info—so who knows whether it is true."

I responded by email within half an hour: "I need a lawyer in Philly ASAP. Can you give me any advice on that?"

Most of the Philadelphia firms could not represent me because they either had business ties with Wyeth or they were already involved in the fen-phen litigation. It took me almost two weeks to find a qualified lawyer who was available to represent me.

Immediately after recovering from the shock of the recent RICO threats, I met with several lawyers I had known from Strasburger and Price, the firm that hired me straight out of law school. Dave Parham was a bankruptcy specialist and Randy Mathis was an experienced civil trial lawyer. Together we began compiling a list of everyone I needed to hire: a bankruptcy lawyer, an asset protection lawyer, and a criminal lawyer. I also decided to hire a Civil RICO specialist in Dallas as well as the one I had recently found in Philadelphia.

The thought of defending a Civil RICO lawsuit while also trying to protect assets and avoid bankruptcy was completely new to me. My divorce lawyer referred me to Jim Mincey, an estate planner who was "the best in the business."

I pulled in the parking lot at Three Forest One Place the following Tuesday morning. The sign just off the elevator read "Kroney/Mincey, L.L.P." *It figures they'd have a bunch of letters after their firm name*, I thought as I exited the elevator.

Herb, my divorce lawyer, had already arrived and was sitting in an easy chair sipping coffee. I greeted him and took a seat. "You're going to like Jim Mincey," Herb said, a bit too cheerfully, but then Herb was always upbeat. Before I could answer, his cell phone rang and he stepped out into the hall, leaving me alone with my thoughts. Just three years earlier, Herb brought estate planning and tax lawyers to my office after my big wins on fen-phen Round One. Here I was now, holding my own crumpled business card with Mincy's address and the words "Asset Protection/bankruptcy advice" written in a nervous scrawl on the back. I stared at those four words as I waited for either of my two absent lawyers to rescue me. Herb prodded my arm; he had been talking to me for a while, but I had been daydreaming.

"Kip! Mincey can see us now."

I followed Herb into a small conference room across from the waiting area. We had just settled into two of the four seats when Jim Mincey nudged the door open. He was an awkward sight. He balanced a large, full coffee cup in one hand and a blank legal pad in the other. I waited for the coffee to slosh out of the cup. Mincey greeted us both somewhat loudly, introduced himself with a pleasant nod and tossed his legal pad toward the two remaining seats, all without spilling so much as a drop. My thoughts bordered on the ridiculous. He was confident, happy, and full of energy. If it had been me, I thought, that coffee would be all over the place. He shook my hand, smiled and looked me in the eye without being judgmental, and within seconds, I realized it wasn't a matter of disliking the man. I envied him for not being me, for not being in my shoes.

Mincey appeared much younger than I had expected. I had assumed that someone who commanded such respect from Herb would be older. But he was my age or younger, tan, physically fit, and sporting a shock of prematurely gray hair more rumpled than the early hour warranted. He had rolled up the sleeves on his blue shirt, and his red tie loosely circled the unbuttoned collar.

When the small talk ended, he produced a pen, adjusted his legal pad and got down to business. "Herb explained that you've been doing great on some type of pharmaceutical cases, but now you're worried that you might be getting sucked into some legal problems," he said. When put that simply, it sounded better than it had in my daydreams.

Aware I was paying by the hour for both attorneys, I briefly explained that I was innocent. "Everyone who knows me knows that, but I'm also realistic. Can I do anything to protect what little I have left, and can I avoid bankruptcy?" I thought money was the purpose of the meeting. After all, "asset protection/bankruptcy advice" were the four words scribbled on the back of the card. He put down his pen, looked up over the top of his reading glasses and stared directly into my eyes.

"Bankruptcy," he said in a very serious tone, "shouldn't be your top concern, Kip. Losing your law license ... going to prison ... there are far worse outcomes for you, in my opinion."

I suddenly hated him again.

He continued, "Mass defection of clients and referring lawyers, thousands of clients suing—that's a hell of a lot worse than filing a quick bankruptcy and then moving on with your life. Besides, in a case like this, all anyone would have to do is allege fraud and they get around the bankruptcy laws." He paused and tapped a firm finger on the stack of documents in front of him and asked, "So, Kip, are you ready to fight this?"

It would be the first of many meetings with Jim. Whether I liked what he had to say or not, I could count on him to be brutally honest. I was in the midst of war, and there would be no time or energy for anything else.

I sat at my desk with pen in hand, staring numbly at the two-sentence agreement Wayne asked me to sign. Weeks earlier, he had both called and emailed, warning about the threats of Civil RICO, sending me scrambling to find an attorney because it was not his area of specialization. Now he was the guy demanding a doubling of his fee. The timing was suspicious and the demand outrageous. If I refused, Wayne would quit, and, according to the agreement, he would still get his five percent. On top of that, I would have to pay someone else another five percent—or maybe more—to be local counsel. And who would want to sign on as local counsel with someone who was in as much trouble as I appeared to be? Either way, I was looking at ten percent or more, and Wayne knew it.

I began to understand "Stockholm Syndrome," the unthinkable manner in which hostages sometimes become loyal to their kidnappers. Confusion, loss of trust and power, and manipulation—these things forced me to need Wayne. Fen-phen was all about deadlines, and the longer I delayed, the more things would pile up, so I stopped fighting him and reluctantly doubled Wayne's fee.

Rumors had been circulating for weeks about lawyers for the Trust harassing echo technicians and witnesses. I then received three calls in two weeks from echo techs who worked for my firm during the screening period, turning rumors to reality.

Lawyers for the Trust showed up on Ed Padua's doorstep toward the end of October. "I told them I measured everything accurately," he said, "and that I was told not to cheat at all." He defended the firm because, according to him, we went out of our way to do everything right. Ed told his visitors he was specifically instructed, "If it is nineteen percent, then call it nineteen percent. Don't ever call it twenty if you think it is nineteen." He said our group had dismissed techs who were too aggressive and that if anyone had anything bad to say about my firm, it was probably out of resentment.

Two other technicians recounted similar visits, and, like Ed, assured me they had nothing but good things to say about our echo program. These three calls, while somewhat alarming, actually reassured me. I had done nothing wrong, and unless the Trust's investigators could convince someone to lie, they would continue to come up empty.

At that moment, it occurred to me that the hell I had been experiencing, the RICO rumor and Scheff's goons, had all been part of the attrition Zimroth had threatened at the settlement meetings in Dallas and New York. They were trying to discourage doctors from helping us, and now they were making unannounced calls on odd days and at odd times, even late into the evening. If they could spook me, and maybe a few others like me, then thousands of claims might never get filed, thus attrition.

🏛

I was on my way home from a strategy session regarding the EchoMotion motions, a clump of threats that could wipe out all tests performed by EchoMotion, seriously damaging almost half of my clients' cases. Wayne was there, and between him and the stress of the meeting, my head was pounding. I was eager to get the kids and then go home and relax.

My phone rang. It was from the 409 area code—Beaumont. I answered. "Jim, buddy!"

"Kip, you were the first person I wanted to call. They came back with a nice verdict this afternoon in the range of $1.36 million. It's a great day in the U.S. of A., and I really wanted to thank you."

We had heard about Jim Morris's verdict at the meeting earlier in the day, but I didn't interrupt. He wanted to tell me himself, and it would take my mind off the traffic that was shaving minutes off my time with my kids. "The boys in Houston were telling me I couldn't handle this on my own—pressuring me to take the little bit Wyeth offered—but it was you and Walter Umphrey who said I could do it.

Thanks, man, and I really mean it."

Jim and I had spoken several times before and during his trial, but this call, especially on the heels of his big win, made me proud. We talked all the way home. I ended the call, smiling from ear to ear, as I pulled into the kids' driveway to pick them up for the weekend.

Linnea and Rendon had just thrown their backpacks onto their beds and run out the back door of my house when a reporter called from the *Wall Street Journal*. "Always happy to talk to the media," I said, positioning my lawn chair in a sunny spot. The two golden retrievers pounced on Linnea, and the three of them rolled in the grass. Rendon joined in the fun, and I turned my attention to the reporter, glad to finally be sharing in good news once again.

FOURTEEN

ONE BEATING AFTER ANOTHER

I FLEW TO Tulsa to talk with some techs that had worked in the Trust's official screening program and left two hours later with signed affidavits from some of their top sonographers. Kim Benzel had more than twenty years experience in performing ultrasound exams and a long and quite impressive list of registrations and certifications. Her affidavit confirmed my suspicions that the Trust had not provided the level of echo supervision that it was now demanding of us.

When word got out that we were collecting affidavits, they poured in from doctors and lawyers I had never even met. The support was phenomenal. There were even several from doctors who had performed echos for the AHP Settlement Trust Screening Program. On January 26, 2004, we filed over one hundred affidavits in opposition to the Trust's motions to disqualify unsupervised echos.

While I reveled in my accomplishment, Wayne took the opportunity to explore the negative. "I've seen lots of pretty looking affidavits from experts with long résumés, but none of that does any good unless that expert holds up well and looks good in court. You got an expert for court, Kip?" He asked.

"No, Wayne," I replied, deflated. "Not yet."

He picked up steam. "What we've got is a federal judge who wants to do the right thing, but what he sees troubles him. He has a company in front of him willing to pay four billion dollars if people are sick. Sure, there's the issue of the word 'supervision' buried somewhere in the bowels of the thousand-page legal document, but Fishbein and Scheff and Wyeth will defend it. At a bare minimum, you need to have every doctor who supervised your echos testify about it live in court if you want to have any hope of overcoming the supervision objections."

"Thanks, Wayne. Always nice talking to you."

Wayne's warnings, as pessimistic and unwelcome as they were, held a lot of truth. Despite our differences, his cynicism would ultimately serve me better than my optimism would.

Bill collectors began lining up at my door as fen-phen payments lagged further and further behind. From the bottom of the barrel—the one people crawl into when the shit is hitting the fan—I occasionally found the courage to peek out the top to see if the coast was clear. Every time I did, the fan was slinging more filth my way. Out of self-preservation, I sank lower and lower. *Please, God, let this finally be the bottom.*

Then Wayne called one Sunday morning in late January 2004.

"It's an article in today's *Philadelphia Inquirer*. I'm faxing it right over," he said.

I saw the title, bold and black, as it clicked teasingly over the fax in my office: "Lawyers: Drug Test Is Target of Fraud."

The article reported that the Trust and Wyeth believed that most of the claims in the Settlement Trust were "bogus" and based on "fraud." It also described how Richard Scheff, Special Counsel to the Trust, had "in a spate of actions" sued "two cardiologists—one of whom he accused of racketeering—and sought to suspend all claims linked to EchoMotion." Then something really caught my attention. "Last week, Scheff set his sights on Dallas lawyer Kip A. Petroff, one of the most active diet drug lawyers in the country. Scheff asked Bartle to suspend all Petroff claims—estimated at seven thousand—filed with the Trust. Scheff contended that Petroff ran his own echocardiogram service, performing thousands of tests—unsupervised—on diet-drug clients ... Petroff, who was not directly accused of any wrongdoing in Scheff's action, did not respond to requests for comment last week ... Scheff has not, as yet, sued any diet-drug lawyer."

Wyeth's lawyer, Peter Zimroth, was quoted as declaring in court filings that the claims process had been "'hijacked by lawyers stamping out tens of thousands of baseless claims' and operating on a scale 'beyond anything that could have been imagined.'" The article went on to note that "Much of the suspected fraud involves echocardiogram tests required to support claims of severe heart-valve damage ... plaintiffs lawyers recruited clients through advertising, set up medical testing 'mills' to conduct echocardiograms en masse, and then paid cardiologists millions of dollars to fill out claim forms listing exaggerated injuries."

I read the article several times that Sunday. What troubled me most was that Wyeth and the Trust were equating unsupervised echos with fraud. The law states that fraud must be coupled with intent to deceive. I was sure Scheff and Wyeth knew that. The thought of anyone believing I set out to commit fraud with our echos was unimaginable, but it looked like that was exactly what Scheff had "set his sights on" trying to prove.

The core allegation, that doctors were paid millions to read hotel echos, was the scariest part of the story. And it was true. Although the echos and readings that followed were done to Trust standards and to general medical standards, the facts had been twisted and contorted until they sounded dirty.

What else were we to have done? The Nationwide Settlement required readings of each echo, and a reading was a billable medical service. What the article failed to say was that the Trust, like the attorneys, also paid millions to have their echos read.

I suspected the story was another example of ghostwriting. Regardless, after enduring one beating after another, I found myself thrust into a new phase in my life. I was waiting to be criminally charged for something that was not a crime.

This had to be the bottom of the barrel.

I got down on my knees and prayed—for the nightmares to stop, for the threats to end. I prayed harder than ever, and when I opened my eyes, I realized I had fallen asleep. I was exhausted and empty and too tired to keep waiting for God to answer my prayers.

Instead, I began my nightly routine long before five o'clock. After pouring progressively taller vodkas, I read the article again hoping it would sound less awful. It did not.

FIFTEEN

RUTHLESS

BECAUSE THE MOTIONS could wipe out, delay, or diminish claim payments, I made the difficult choice to tell clients that they might be better off finding a safer attorney. Client newsletters had always been one of my favorite duties. Folks appreciated being informed, and that made my life easier. But this was different than anything I had ever written. It read like a confession.

I considered also telling clients about the rumored RICO threats, but my ethics advisor, Lynn Baker, stopped me. "There's a fine line between telling clients when bad things have actually happened and when you think something bad might happen. Those rumors started months ago and still nothing. Now they're trying to sweat one of you out by turning up the heat. Listen, these lawyers want to make everyone squirm in the hopes that one of you will turn against the others and make the Trust's case for them. Don't let them spook you."

The letter was written, printed, and ready to be signed. A cheap blue Paper Mate pen sat like a tombstone over my printed name. I signed the letter and handed it to Redonda without a word.

My message had been clear: Petroff and Associates was in big trouble, but my clients might be able to avoid problems if they fired me and hired a new lawyer. We were aware that we were inviting them to abandon us, but it was the only ethical thing to do. Despite my assurance to readers that our clients' echocardiograms had been "properly supervised, professionally acquired, and are medically reliable," it was hard to miss the letter's gloomy tone.

I tossed the Paper Mate toward the stacks of files on the credenza. It slid behind into the long forgotten collection of dusty Post-It-Notes and paperclips below. *Leave it*, I thought. *Serves it right.*

The next day I watched with a sickening sense of dread as the last mail crate left. Each carried with it the potential loss of a client. Everything I had worked for over the last six and a half years of my life was literally up for grabs, and I had done nothing wrong. Wyeth's hurtful tactics, and later the Trust's claims practices, had made victims of my clients, and now their legal manipulations were doing the same to me. My firm had become one of fen-phen's most notable insurgents, so I was the target of Wyeth's and the Trust's strongest, most desperate retaliations.

Vance had helped me muddle through the various drafts of the letter and would support me no matter what. I needed some words of wisdom.

"Who the hell they gonna go to if they decide to leave you anyway?" he asked, referring to my clients. "Everyone's in the same boat as you, right?"

I wished it was that easy. "Yeah," I said, "But no one in the country, no one, has the honor of being implicated in all of the current motions. That is a distinction that Yours Truly shares alone, Vance." He said nothing. He cleared his throat and seemed to fumble for what to say next.

"I doubt we'll get much sympathy from Bartle when it comes down to either making us billionaires or saving the local drug company."

"No kidding." I had always felt this unshakable confidence in the courtroom—the ability to get into character, win the jury's trust and present my client in a sympathetic light. But Judge Bartle was not a jury; he was a judge—a United States District Judge—holding court just one county east of where Wyeth resided. I had dragged the Yankee drug company through Texas courts, but now this was very different. These same people were his neighbors, and we were the outsiders. It was unlikely he would suddenly feel sympathetically toward a Texas plaintiff's attorney with multiple motions already filed against him.

"You'll probably lose some clients," Vance warned, "and you might even have some lawyers take out blocks of cases." Blocks of cases were more like icebergs large enough to sink the Titanic. Herrman and Herrman easily had a thousand cases with me, as did the "Oklahoma Consortium" and Frenkel and Frenkel and the numbers kept mounting. "But most people will stick with you," Vance insisted.

I breathed deeply and slowly. "You really think so, Vance?"

"Hell, yeah, Kip! People know you. They respect you, man. They're going to be loyal because that's the smart thing to do here. It might be a bit rough, but most of them wouldn't know how to handle these cases on their own, and all the lawyers who would know what to do with them have their hands full with their own cases. Relax. We're going to be okay."

It had been a full month since the Sunday morning *Philadelphia Inquirer* article about Scheff "setting his sights" on me, and there still were no new lawsuits. Very few clients or partnering attorneys seemed concerned about my dreaded newsletter and the spate of motions. And none fired me. I was beginning to think Scheff had given up after hearing so many good things about my echo program from the witnesses his lawyers had spoken to last year. Then, on February 24, 2004, I received a call from a former echo technician, John Coningsby.

"I got home about an hour ago, and I saw these two men sitting in a car," he explained. "It seemed strange at the time, it being pretty cold up here this time of year, but I didn't pay much attention. I barely stepped out of my car when they walked right up to me. They weren't from around here. They were wearing dark suits and long trench coats—stiff-like. They looked kind of like those guys in *Men in Black*."

"What'd they say?" I asked, giving him a chance to catch his breath.

"The one guy handed me his card. I've got it right here. Scott Coffina from Montgomery McCracken. You know them?"

I did. It was Richard Scheff's law firm, and these were, no doubt, his henchmen. "Trust lawyers."

John said they apologized for interrupting dinner, that they were almost military in their manner and that they wanted answers about echos. "This Coffina guy was kind of scary—real intimidating. It seems my echos, the ones I did for you, are under some kind of investigation. I explained I did the echos for you the way I did them for everyone else, and no one else had any problems with them."

"That all?" My mind had drifted to the ice-cold glass waiting for me in the kitchen.

"No. He said, 'Maybe you'd feel more comfortable talking if you had your own attorney.' Then he offered to hire me one, so I said, 'Why do I need an attorney?' I was mad, man, but he acted all impatient, like I was the one wasting his time. Shoot, my dinner was getting cold! I told 'em 'Listen, guys, I don't know what you're getting at, but these folks, they're on top of things. I learned a lot from working with them. And our echos—regardless what you and your people think—they're the best.' They weren't all that interested, so I added something like, 'Kip ran a tight ship. Our echos had to be better than even the hospital's.' They really didn't say much after that. Guess they wanted dirt, and I wouldn't give them any, so they left. I'd have called you sooner, but my dinner was getting cold."

The Trust had forty "time keepers," paralegals and lawyers billing the Trust by the hour. Together, they ran the Claims Integrity Program, a broad title affording Scheff virtually unlimited reach. The men in black, the ones who visited John and some of our other echo techs, were Scheff's investigators. He needed them to justify his outrageous budget. I wondered how many echo techs and other potential witnesses they had talked to. *Maybe the only ones who call me are the ones who liked us*, I thought. There were at least a couple dozen; now I had heard from four. *Why haven't the rest called me?*

🏛

It was not enough that the Trust or Scheff or Wyeth's defense team were damaging the reputations of plaintiffs' attorneys. They were determined to go after anyone who supported them, even if it meant cutting off their own noses.

Donna Dicken was a Trust employee who liked a little attention. She got that from frustrated attorneys on the outside because, unlike most Trust workers, Donna promptly returned calls and made notable progress on otherwise stagnant files. This made her very popular. When a plaintiffs' lawyer stated openly and innocently enough in court that he had talked to Donna, he had not realized that she had been acting in secret and that his statement would give the Trust a new apparatus for their campaign of terror. Thirteen attorneys were subpoenaed in connection with the Dicken investigation, including two of my employees and myself. The Trust brought a team of lawyers to Dallas for a series of depositions. Their investigation yielded little, but their message was clear: The Trust was not in the business of being friendly.

Donna Dicken learned that lesson the hard way. She lost her job and endured repeated interrogations. She was probably never in a position to, nor did she intend to, hurt the Trust. She was just a nice lady, sacrificed to make a point.

SIXTEEN

_____ ⛫ _____

THE SEVENTH AMENDMENT

THE ORIGINAL SETTLEMENT Agreement had not clearly provided for what would happen if the Trust ran out of money. And despite Scheff's efforts to force attrition, the threat of "busting the trust" was becoming a reality—a reality that could leave Wyeth vulnerable to bankruptcy.

So in late 2003 and early 2004, a new deal that would limit its mounting potential payout was discussed. Wyeth needed some assurance that the plaintiffs would accept it, and plaintiffs' lawyers, tired of dodging bullets, were interested in hearing a less nerve-racking alternative. Changes to class action settlements are called amendments, and since this would be the seventh change, Wyeth's proposal would be called the Seventh Amendment or 7A.

Wayne Spivey and Jerry Alexander were the principal lawyers who negotiated its early terms, serving as liaisons throughout the negotiations. As members of the Seventh Amendment Liaison Committee, their roles would eventually become very similar to Class Counsel's role on the original four billion dollar deal. None of us realized at the time that this would pose a conflict of interest for Wayne. He would eventually be working at Fishbein's side, along with Wyeth, while still working for me. Because I had more cases than anyone else in the country, any deal involving near-unanimous consent would need my clients' backing. So they tried to keep me in the loop from the beginning.

According to the initial groundwork, it seemed 7A would be fair and prompt. In exchange, Wyeth would commit $1.275 billion to a "Supplemental Settlement Fund," which was basically a new pot of money for those willing to go into the new deal and abandon the original deal. All claimants had to agree to it. Those not in agreement could stay in the original settlement and take their chances with Scheff's Claims Integrity Program.

One key provision guaranteed Wyeth would have "walk-away rights," permitting it to leave the new deal if too many claimants rejected it. This would allow Wyeth to see if full participation could be garnered without first having to legally commit to the deal. It would only be an acceptable settlement if all (or nearly all) claimants in the old deal agreed to go into the new deal.

It certainly sounded more appealing than the current Trust, so I offered my support, but that was not enough. Wayne and Jerry needed me to promote it.

Getting clients to buy into the Seventh Amendment had been fairly easy. For the most part, we had shielded them from the Trust's machinations, and they seemed to trust my judgment. But many fellow attorneys were still reeling from their own experiences with the Trust and needed time to carefully consider any new arrangement.

Wayne finally reached the end of his rope. Fed up with the dissidents and their "whining," he threatened to back out of negotiations, sarcastically suggesting that those who "filled the Matrix with meritless claims" continue bargaining with Judge Bartle.

The "meritless" claims were the very ones I had entrusted him to help resolve for the past eighteen months. Had he really been working on behalf of those clients if he considered their claims meritless? I wondered how I could count on him to represent their interests in the future, and I wondered what had been said about them to Fishbein, the man in charge of paying them.

Wayne Spivey had taken off the gloves. Either I got the rest of the holdouts onboard, or Wayne was backing out and Fishbein would come after my clients and my firm. Despite how I felt about Wayne or Fish, the new deal was our best option. Yes, Wayne was way out of line, but I had to go with what I knew was best for the clients. By the middle of summer 2004, the Seventh Amendment was submitted to Judge Bartle for approval. There were still some who objected, but Wyeth was willing to proceed as long as we continued our recruitment efforts.

While everyone else seemed to have reason to want the new deal, Scheff had every reason to oppose it. If the Seventh Amendment was approved, he could be out of a job. So Scheff, on behalf of the Trust, refused to endorse it.

I sat at my desk the morning of June 15, 2004, staring blankly at Scheff's newest weapon—a fax. It was accompanied by several identical documents that Redonda had received from fellow attorneys and a couple of doctors. They were tolling agreements that offered to extend the statute of limitations, if signed, so the Trust could sue the recipient later. The thought of being sued sickened me, so I stood still waiting for the uneasiness to pass. In that quiet moment it occurred to me that the document had been oddly vague. The agreement should have specified the nature of the limitation being tolled, which it failed to do. It was an open-ended agreement to let Scheff sue us for anything he wanted whenever he wanted. If signed, it could have been lethal.

Two of the copies had been sent to Dr. Waenard Miller and Dr. Robert Rosenthal who had served as experts for us in the past. They were sent to the doctors in such haste and amidst such confusion that their names had been filled in next to the word "lawyer." Scheff had hoped to come at us quickly from every direction, causing confusion and tricking us into doing something we would later regret. Instead, we basically ignored the agreements while never again giving Scheff the benefit of the doubt.

As the weeks passed, there were no lawsuits against those who refused to sign, but there was also no relief from the threat of Civil RICO that had been skulking about for the past year.

Then the Trust made a move. It sent letters to my co-counsel suggesting that they could accelerate their own progress by canceling their deal with my firm. The only action the lawyer had to take was to complete a Source of Echo form disavowing any association with me on certain claims pending before the Trust. Once the form was returned, delayed claims would then be put back in the queue for processing.

Signing the Source of Echo form could be an appealing option. It would distance the attorney from me professionally, thus buffering him from the threats aimed my way. For those with whom I had a working arrangement, this would force me to forfeit my portion of joint damages. But it also meant the signing attorney would have to go to battle against an increasingly aggressive Trust on his own. To my knowledge, not a single lawyer chose to jump ship. And despite the poor timing of the Trust's letter, most plaintiffs' lawyers eventually agreed to support the Seventh Amendment.

🏛

One type of Matrix claim that many lawyers thought had been beyond the Trust's destructive reach were the high level claims or cases involving surgery, very serious medical problems, or death. The problem for many of these claimants was that some received only the lawyer-sponsored echo during the screening period, and these were now being called into question. They had echos taken at their cardiologists' offices later confirming what our early tests found, but those were not sufficient to support the claims because they happened after the screening deadline.

One such client's claim had been pending without action for months when we contacted Scheff to inquire about its status. Scheff responded that the claim was supported by an unsupervised echo and that the Trust would be violating the Settlement Agreement by paying it. It had been put "on hold."

We then began replacing hotel echos with echos taken in doctors' offices during the screening period. This would cause a delay in payment, but the echos (while the same quality) would be less disputable and improved our chances of getting a fair settlement. The delay ate up all our cash reserves, so with the firm broke again we took our fight to the courtroom. It was our last remaining hope to keep the firm alive until there was some progress on the Matrix claims.

This time the trials would be on their turf, and the rules would not be in our favor. And our biggest hammer, the threat of punitive damages, was gone forever.

SEVENTEEN

GOING THE DISTANCE

THE SUMMER OF 2004 marked the beginning of a season of important, Round Two benchmark trials. We were in Philadelphia state court because that was where Wyeth's corporate headquarters were located, and suing them there allowed us to stay in state court and avoid all the delays and problems associated with the Federal MDL. That was the good part. The bad part was that we were in Wyeth's hometown, and the citizens of Philadelphia County (including the judges and jurors) would be skeptical of our attacks on one of their local companies. The future of over 50,000 opt-out cases depended on what happened in these courtrooms.

The Houston firms had teams of lawyers and paralegals working long hours in Philadelphia prepping their various trial teams. They rented several conference rooms and nearly a dozen regular rooms at the hotel across from the county courthouse, and these became satellite offices and home to the fen-phen libraries—six years of accumulated documents. It was everything a lawyer trying a fen-phen case could possibly need, and Robert and I had been the ones to help sow the original seeds.

Most of these cases would be tried under the reverse bifurcation system that had been used for years in Philadelphia asbestos trials. The first phase of the trial asks the jury if fen-phen caused the injury, and if the answer is yes, how much money should be awarded. If they answered yes and awarded damages, then the second phase would consist of asking the jury to decide if Wyeth was liable for the injury.

In more traditional trials, liability and damages are considered alongside one another. If bifurcated at all, liability is usually decided first and causation and damages are considered second. Reverse bifurcation completely eliminates the possibility of enraging a jury, since the company's conduct is only discussed after causation is decided and damages assessed. These first few that had been chosen to go to trial were test cases, which meant we would use the results as benchmarks to measure the value of all of our similar cases. Now that we could not seek punitive damages, we needed a new baseline to assess what juries thought the remaining cases were worth. This might allow us to come to an agreeable settlement with Wyeth without having to take each one to trial.

Our first test case in the bifurcated system was awarded fifty thousand dollars and was settled without even going into the liability phase. The other received forty-eight thousand a few weeks later—not exactly earth shattering results. Still, they were better than other firms' test cases, which received less or resulted in defense verdicts, meaning Wyeth was not liable and no damages were awarded.

The ugly truth was starting to become clear: trying all of our opt-outs would be too expensive if these low dollar verdicts were representative of the outcomes because the cost of trying the cases exceeded the damages being awarded. It had been comparatively easy when we could flash the impressive bad conduct evidence, as we had done in Debbie Lovett's trial. Without it, we were stymied. I had underestimated the powerful threat of punitive damages and assumed I could still reap impressive rewards without them.

GOING THE DISTANCE

Judges began losing patience. They did not want to clog their dockets with hundreds of cases that averaged under fifty thousand dollars per verdict. We were feeling less than welcome in the City of Brotherly Love.

Our luck seemed to change in mid-October. Wyeth sent word they wanted to discuss settling my trial-scheduled cases and a few others that were in varying stages of readiness around the country. After several meetings were cancelled, I began to think they were toying with me. After all, my recent court victories were not exactly intimidating them.

Finally, we met. It was odd from the start. I was the only one who seemed to have my head in the game. Wyeth attorney Ellen Reisman kept checking her watch, and Wayne, normally the uptight one, was far too calm and casual. I had the feeling I could have demanded any amount, and after a late start and some effortless negotiating, they proved me right. We settled our tiny cluster of cases that day for fourteen million dollars. It was far more than I expected and exceeded what they had previously been willing to pay on similar cases.

Back at the office, I shared the news with Stan, who had been up to his ears in trial preparation. The settlement freed his time significantly and provided the cash needed to keep the firm in business. We were in the midst of football season, and I thought briefly about buying tickets. But there were bigger priorities. We still had about four thousand potential 7A cases pending in our office alone and a couple thousand with co-counsel nationwide. They had been in the Matrix since 2003, and now they were going into the new deal. Thirty seven hundred of those were ready to go, but our conference room was piled high with about three hundred deficiencies, claims that had some problem that needed to be resolved in order to be considered for the Seventh Amendment. We had just six weeks to complete the job, and it would take almost every man-hour to meet our deadline.

145

By August 2004, Judge Bartle had granted preliminary trial court approval for the Seventh Amendment. The court would send official notices directly to Matrix clients with more information and offering an opt-out deadline of November 9, 2004. The official court notice summarized the new deal in sixty or so cumbersome pages. It had the potential to be overwhelming, so we prepared a "summary of the summary" in the form of an eight-page letter.

Our summary message was that the current Trust was failing clients and that the Seventh Amendment would serve them better. But we warned our clients that they could be leaving a system where a "Matrix claim was valued at approximately four hundred-twenty thousand dollars on average" to one where "each such claim will have a value under the Seventh Amendment of approximately sixty-eight thousand, on average." In other words, claimants could hold out for more money and possibly end up with nothing under the Trust or improve their chances greatly and accept a smaller payment under the new deal.

Our attempts to clarify the court document did little to alleviate the misinformation that infected the fen-phen community. Clients gathered in droves at online message boards and spread rumors that resulted in panic, confusion and downright rebellion. With Wayne and Jerry constantly holding a Wyeth walkout over our heads, my firm and I spent hours trying to put rumors and objections to rest.

"We think they're probably going to go through with it," Wayne's voice crackled over the speakerphone when I asked about the status of the new deal just days before the walk-away deadline. "But Wyeth still likes to whine about the amount, and they constantly bitch about the fraudulent hotel echos and how these people's claims would probably get thrown out if they kept fighting in court."

Jerry added, "There are still those who want them to fight these bogus claims no matter how long it takes and no matter how ugly it gets."

"They can complain all they want," I said. "But they're getting off cheap, and they know it."

"If," he stressed, and then stressed again, "*If* they take the deal. It's not finalized yet," Jerry cautioned.

There was just a little too much smugness in his voice—a little too much lecture and not enough teamwork.

"Look," I said, heatedly. "I feel sorry for you two. You've been put in a really tough position and have had to put up with a lot of whining, complaining, and finger pointing, but I'm sick of hearing how good Wyeth has it and how I ought to kiss their criminal asses. You seem to forget that their lies and manipulations started this whole mess. Six million people put their trust in this drug company. Wyeth is NOT the victim. Our clients are!"

I waited for either of them to argue, but they just listened, so I continued. "The Seventh Amendment is a good deal, and I hope it goes through, but for your sake, not mine. If honesty and justice account for anything, my clients are going to be okay, deal or no deal, even if it takes a decade of court battles."

Jerry managed, "Wyeth paints a much different picture. They're still holding out hope Judge Bartle will grant the current motions, too, and they won't stop there. Some docs' Green Forms could be rejected altogether, and lawyers and firms who abused the system," he paused, clearing his throat, "could be expelled from representing any claimants. And there is still talk about claimants paying a deposit to cover the Trust's audit costs for rejects." I could imagine Fishbein silently passing a note to Wayne just as I had seen him pass notes to the Trust and Wyeth during the Crouse hearings. He would support whatever ridiculous measure Wyeth proposed.

Wayne took up where Jerry left off. "Plus, Scheff and Wyeth always threaten their so-called 'recovery actions' that might recall some of the early claims payments. They love to remind us about that."

"Listen, guys, I'm sick of being lumped in with a bunch of lawyers and doctors and echo techs who might have gotten caught going a little over the speed limit!"

Jerry was all too happy to chime in. "They say you are the worst one—that you ran a bogus shop. And they think they can knock you out completely by the time the first few motions are heard. Sorry to be so blunt, but that's what we hear when we listen to Wyeth talk about the landscape of a future without the Seventh Amendment."

So it all came down to this: I either finished rallying support for 7A, or my head was on the chopping block. I paced the office that afternoon, staring out the eleventh floor window, wondering how I ended up here. I tried doing everything right, but my conduct was in question. Where had things gone so wrong? The possibility of the motions and trials ahead was frightening. Wyeth was a gargantuan machine that could crush me with countless lawyers and unlimited time and resources. Wyeth, with the Trust's help, was using the same tactic against me that I had used against them in Round One: back-to-back court dates had overwhelmed Wyeth and pressured them to settle. The threat of more of the same was what caused Wyeth to agree to the Nationwide Settlement. Now it was Wyeth that seemed to have overwhelmed the plaintiffs' attorneys—me especially—with back-to-back motions and threats.

The Wall Street Journal had once slightly embellished my cases, giving me credit for a hundred when I really only had fifty. At that time, I remember thinking how I wished I had hundreds, or even thousands. Now I had thousands and longed for simpler times.

Wyeth's walk-away deadline came and went, and they chose not to exercise that option. But it was around this time that a study found that approximately seventy percent of claims that originally passed audit should not have done so. The Trust announced it would be retraining its auditors so that they could better detect fraud and deceptive sonographic techniques in claims. Here we were again, plowing old ground rather than making progress on the claims.

The Trust was no longer accusing just plaintiffs' attorneys and a few scattered doctors. They were seeing fraud everywhere they looked. Their newest targets were well-respected doctors throughout the country who had originally signed Green Forms supporting Matrix claims. These professionals' opinions had been respected when the Trust's auditors approved over a thousand early studies, and trained auditors had agreed then that the echos qualified for Matrix benefits. Now that there were more claims than expected, the Trust decided the various doctors' embedded fraud had been so sophisticated that they had fooled even the auditors. Hundreds of claims that had already been approved, but not paid, would have to be re-examined. Payments were, again, on hold.

If trained doctors and auditors missed the alleged fraud when they initially reviewed the files, how was an attorney, one with no medical training, supposed to have detected it? Because, in their minds, it had been my scam all along. And I was so convincing that dozens of squeaky-clean techs, attorneys, paralegals, and doctors gave up their honest careers to join me.

It was a ridiculous piece of fiction, but it was easier than admitting that they had put together a deal that had never made mathematical sense. The Trust never had enough money to satisfy all the claims, so they concocted schemes to create attrition despite the fact they were destroying careers and lives in the process.

The earlier reverse bifurcation test trials in the summer of 2004 produced wins and losses for both sides, but nothing truly remarkable occurred. Then, in Philadelphia, two women who claimed Pondimin caused their heart valve leakage received a record two hundred million dollar verdict. This raised the benchmark for all similar pending cases including a chunk of my own. Wyeth and I were amidst negotiations, and on July 1, 2005, we settled all five hundred of our remaining opt-outs for about twenty-five million dollars. After years of fighting, we were finally nearing the end.

Peter Grossi, one of the Arnold and Porter lawyers who had earned my full respect in his defense of Wyeth, sent me an email. In the subject line were two words: The End. He wrote, "I understand you reached an agreement today on your remaining cases. Congratulations. It's been over seven years since I met you on these cases. You have been a worthy opponent. I wish you well. Grossi."

We had gone the distance, and I had made it out alive. On top of all that, my opponent was congratulating me after years of relentless torture. I took a deep breath and closed my eyes.

Peace.

There was finally peace for almost all my opt-out clients. But for my Matrix clients, the war raged on.

EIGHTEEN

FRIENDS, FOES & FISH

EN-PHEN HAD BLEMISHED my professional reputation. I was eager to leave this chapter of my existence behind so I could find my way back to happiness. But to get Wyeth out of my life, I had to change the minds of objectors to the Seventh Amendment. It was very rewarding, almost therapeutic, and a lot like spring cleaning. I worked my way down a list, checking off each group or individual who agreed to withdraw his or her objections, methodically clearing a path to allow my own clients safe passage and to ensure my peace.

Judge Bartle issued final trial court approval on March 15, 2005, formally approving the amendment. This obligated Wyeth to deposit fifty million dollars into the Seventh Amendment Alternative Claims Facility. That money was used to begin administering the new deal and to begin a medical review of each individual claim.

The way was now clear for the last stage, final judicial approval. Before the judge would issue that, however, all appeals had to be resolved. Robert Bishop and Karen Hogan, the only two remaining holdouts, now had to take their cases to the Third Circuit Court of Appeals or drop their objections.

Robert Bishop was a seasoned lawyer with a reputation for

representing objectors to class action settlements. He would collect clients with cases that would fall through the cracks or that had some other legal basis for objecting. He would wait until the worst possible moment to object, threatening progress, and he would stick with it until someone paid him to go away. It was exactly what we did, and he officially withdrew his objection.

Karen Hogan was now our only objector, and she seemed to enjoy the attention more than she craved the money. She claimed she did not have a lawyer, but she was all over online message boards corresponding with a mysterious figure known as the "phen fen king." Just as he failed to use proper spelling, he also failed to weigh the consequences of his actions. He allowed Karen Hogan, known online as "Flossy," to believe she was doing something important. Together they shared an intense resentment toward virtually every aspect of the court system in general and the fen-phen Class Action Settlement in particular. We spent an expensive year-and-a-half trying to determine how to get a grip on her while seeking the true identity of the elusive "king."

My next client newsletter was brief, and a little embarrassing, because it highlighted the fact that only one person, a non-lawyer no less, was holding up the entire $1.275 billion deal. Part of my frustration was based on the complex manner in which she was approaching a simple situation. She had no real reason to appeal or object if she did not like the Seventh Amendment. All she had to do was opt out of it. This would have allowed her to maintain her original Matrix claim, and anyone who wanted the Seventh Amendment could have it.

In the meantime, Wyeth was not required to pay any more money into the fund until there was final judicial approval. That meant that, during the delay, the company was earning interest and claimants were losing it daily because of one holdout.

Even more troubling was the fact that the Trust was still lurking in the shadows. It refused to endorse the Seventh Amendment, and we wondered if indictments or the RICO suit were still a threat. Scheff steadfastly contended that Dr. Crouse had committed fraud, and with each day that passed, we wondered if she would, in her desperation, turn on us or try to drag us in.

The EchoMotion motion and all the other related problems were incentive enough to leave the Trust and the constant intimidation. Those going into the Seventh Amendment would be free of the threats, the motions, and the harassment; those remaining in the Trust would still have to deal with Scheff and his tactics. With each day of delay, something—anything—could derail our progress before the next big hurdle, final judicial approval.

The Trust and its lawyers had a strong financial interest in stalling. Scheff's ability to instill fear was one of his greatest talents, but the new deal would rob him of his platform. Criminal indictments, which remained a threat, would give the former prosecutor the bloodbath for which he thirsted. Furthermore, this would create the attrition Wyeth so badly needed.

Any delay at all afforded authorities more time to gather evidence to help them with their indictments.

Karen Hogan was a Seventh Amendment opt-out, so objecting would gain her nothing, and it was obvious to everyone but the "king" that she didn't have legal standing. He (or she) continued egging Hogan on with misguided legal advice. Finally, a group of several claimants' attorneys offered her more money than she would get from the Trust to drop her appeal. She agreed, but then she demanded more after she had accepted the offer. On October 24, before she could get paid, the U.S. Third Circuit Court of Appeals ruled against her.

Our problems appeared to finally be over. Hogan's case would go back to the starting line, get audited, and she would then be just like any other claimant. But she continued to drag out her appeal, delaying final judicial approval of the Seventh Amendment. The delay came at a cost (in interest) of fifty thousand dollars a day, a million and a half a month—eighteen million a year.

BATTLING GOLIATH

We suspected that she would wait until the last minute on the date of the deadline to file. The Supreme Court's summer recess was nearing, and its decision would have to be uncharacteristically fast if her appeal hearing was to occur before the break. If not, it would be delayed until the fall.

As expected, Hogan filed at the eleventh hour, and her document needed more work. The clerk rejected it but gave her thirty days to correct the deficiencies and file a new one. This would put her filing deadline near the end of April, and that would all but guarantee that her case would have to wait until after summer recess ended. That meant final judicial approval would not occur until the fall of 2006 at the earliest.

All the while, my clients, and others relying on the Seventh Amendment, hung in limbo. They would never see their money, or the accumulating interest, until Hogan backed down. By this time, she had publicly announced in online message boards that she lost her audit and would receive nothing from the Trust. A small group of plaintiffs' attorneys again offered her a settlement. She eagerly accepted and, as promised, dropped her appeal, thus clearing the path to the Seventh Amendment for the rest of the class.

After all my clients had endured to this point, it was infuriating that one of their own had jeopardized something that would bring closure. The only reason even imaginable for Hogan's actions, at least to me, was that someone had something to gain by stalling the deal. They used a claimant to do their dirty work by firing her up with fear and passion and by making her feel important. The sad truth is that Karen Hogan had been a puppet, and while I had suspicions about who had been pulling her strings, I had no proof to back those suspicions up. Of course, it no longer mattered once Hogan's case was settled, and I never concerned myself about the identity of her puppeteer after that.

Despite the ongoing concerns with the new deal, I had no regrets. Behind me was Scheff, decked out in Reaper's robes and wielding a bloody scythe, and ahead of me was 7A—no friendlier, and certainly no safer, but somehow less frightening. I had convinced my clients and colleagues to put their faith in the new deal. Now that we were there, there was no turning back.

The old fight was over, but there was a new battle ahead that required my full attention. The Seventh Amendment was not all that it had been promised. Some attorneys were seeing even fewer claims successfully exit the processing system than they had while working with the Trust. Mutiny was in the air, and everyone was pointing fingers.

On March 2, 2006, a meeting was scheduled in Philadelphia to update everyone on progress since the new arrangement had been put into place. As one of 7A's advocates, I made plans to attend, but then my friend and colleague, Richard McKennon, died tragically in a motorcycle accident. Wayne and Jerry were understanding when I explained that I needed to stay in Dallas for the funeral. "We have your back," Wayne later emailed.

I sent Carlos Fernandez to the meeting in my place—a young, energetic attorney at my firm who returned from Philadelphia with an impressive stack of detailed notes about what he had seen and heard. I read through the copied packet he gave to me and didn't like what I saw on page nine.

I found Carlos hunkered over his small desk. I hated to interrupt his momentum. He was, undoubtedly, unraveling some twisted conundrum, but this was important.

"Carlos, tell me everything you can remember about these criminal investigations involving the FBI and DOJ." He seemed a little flustered but quickly adapted, turned to page nine in his own perfect packet of notes, and clarified: "The FBI has seized the tape room at the Trust. Nothing goes in or comes out without the FBI approving it. That's probably why getting things from the Trust has become so difficult lately. There was speculation about what that means, but no one is talking if they know."

He went on to explain that FBI agents had unexpectedly visited an elderly claimant's home on a Sunday afternoon. The agents told the woman that her doctor denied prescribing the drugs she said she took in her claim. The claimant had her original signed prescription, but how many people save those types of things? And what might have happened to this woman had she not saved hers? And what drove her doctor to deny prescribing Redux in the first place? Their witch hunt had been fruitless, which should have been a relief. But it was proof that prosecutors were still active, and the FBI was making house calls. That scared me. Scheff's threat of civil RICO seemed minor when compared to the FBI's criminal reach. Scheff could take my money, but the FBI could put me in prison for a long, long time—if they misinterpreted innocent information or were able to convince enough people, like the elderly claimant's doctor, to twist the truth.

I suspected Fishbein was behind the whole thing, acting on behalf of Wyeth, and who knows who else was involved. Wayne even told me as much in an email: "After all, Wyeth is behind all this."

The monster I was fighting had grown many ugly heads. It was Wyeth. It was the Trust, intent on wiping me out. It was Class Counsel (Fish had bragged that he would put us behind bars, and by "us," it seemed he meant me). In fact, Wyeth, my natural enemy, seemed like the least of my concerns.

🏛

Going up against the Fish on his home turf was professional suicide. Opposing him was an open invitation for retaliation. Motions and threats were his weapons of choice. He got a kick out of sending drafts of hotly worded motions, threatening to file them with the judge if we didn't give him what he wanted. Fish even explained this tactic to Judge Bartle, but he conveniently left out the fact that his draft motions were filled with half-truths, untruths, and unfair personal attacks on those who contested the Fishbein Money Machine. But this tactic worked because it was widely perceived that he could get away with it.

Wayne Spivey eventually became Class Counsel's mouthpiece, bringing Mike Fishbein's messages and warnings directly to me. This made Wayne the bad guy and allowed Fish to have some degree of separation from the dirty work, freeing him up to attack me with even greater ferocity.

But I still had my leverage—my bargaining chip. Fish needed my approval to claim his half billion in fees, and I still needed Fish for my clients to learn the results of their claims. The fen-phen Tango was becoming more heated and passionate.

But then Wayne interfered, completely robbing me of my leverage. Wayne sent a copy of Fishbein's Master Fee Agreement requesting five hundred million dollars from the court and instructed me to sign it. When I asked Wayne why Fish, Class Counsel, and the others should be paid before the clients, whom they liked to call greedy and impatient, he explained that it was not up for negotiation. I had not been consulted because he had negotiated on my behalf, and returning to the bargaining table was out of the question. He had thrown in my last chip, my only hope, and now the power was all Fishbein's.

"It would be a lot easier to stomach dealing with Fishbein if he was worrying about the claimants half as much as he is worrying about his fees," I informed Wayne by email.

Fish and his group were presenting a half-billion dollar invoice to be paid in full before the job was complete. He had made basically the same request several years earlier, but the judge had instructed him to first finish the job. Now he had apparently decided he had done enough, despite the fact that too many of my clients' claims were still unpaid. Suspecting he would lose interest in clients after receiving the fee, I had intended to refuse to support the fee agreement until each of my clients received their medical review results. Now, that was not an option.

Wayne insisted that I agree to Fishbein's Petition. He reminded me that Fish was "salivating" at the thought of finally getting to take the gloves off with me in front of Judge Bartle. My continued defiance would delay payments to clients, and the delay, he argued, would be blamed squarely on my opposition.

He then circulated emails to other plaintiffs' lawyers announcing that "Kip intends to sign" knowing I was still strongly opposed. He knew that once I was on board—at least as far as appearances went—those with fewer cases or less confidence would follow suit. I was being used, and I knew it, but at least the result would be that my clients would finally get paid.

Wayne's relationship with Wyeth had clearly changed. After successfully helping me settle my chunks of opt-outs, he got into a rhythm and began offering this service directly to Wyeth. As "Claims Facilitator," he traveled the country working directly with the drug company and its defense team to settle other attorneys' opt-outs, making many millions of dollars in just a few short months. That, in itself, was not scandalous. But what eventually emerged was.

Wayne was sharing sensitive information about clients, information that could seriously and negatively affect the value of claims, with members of the Wyeth defense team. For instance, after undermining and devaluing one client's case in direct correspondence with a Wyeth attorney, Wayne concluded his email by confiding that, "If I ever see Kip again after this litigation is over, it will be too soon." Yet he remained my local Philadelphia attorney and my co-counsel. His loyalty was supposed to have been to our clients and to my firm. Had he given me the same inside scoop on Wyeth that he evidently provided to them in reference to our clients, the outcome might have been very different for the victims of fen-phen.

Wayne Spivey had not seemed the ambitious type. He always said he had my back, and I trusted that for a long while he actually did. And, at points, I had even considered him a friend. But now, he was stabbing me in the back. He had used me for 7A, and he was shoving Fish's fee agreement down my throat as well.

If I refused to sign Fish's fee petition, I would make my point and retain my leverage, but it would be at my clients' expense. If I signed, I would sacrifice my bargaining chip, invite defeat, and make Wayne a hero in Fishbein's eyes. It was not in my character to give up a fight. But I owed it to my clients to accept a ceasefire, and that's what I did in early December of 2006.

NINETEEN

A WELCOME RELIEF

I WAS ANOTHER step closer to the peace I so badly wanted. But if I was ever going to truly achieve it, my personal life needed a little housekeeping first. I had always been a disciplined drinker, if such a person exists. I never drank during work hours and refused to let it interfere with my job. It did, however, start to leave an ugly stain on my personal life. My children, especially Linnea and Leandra, were not as close to me as they had once been, and I was certain my drinking was to blame. Each day I tried to cut back or to start later. Some nights I didn't start until ten or eleven, but I always took that first drink, and after that, the amount was unimportant. With that first drink, I lost any power to resist another and blacked out almost every night. My family meant the world to me. The children were growing up fast, but in my vodka-induced haze, I was missing important parts of their lives.

I quit drinking twice, so I knew it was within my power. But without a drink, settling down each night was tough. The tension from the day would wind tighter and tighter, and I knew that taking one little drink would calm me down enough to sleep. Only, there was no longer such a thing as one little drink.

I would wake up with small, mysterious injuries such as scratches, bruises, or burns, and I had no idea how I had gotten them. These injuries and hangovers were my routine, as were the lies to myself that I would drink less that night. I was consumed with guilt. I was not strong enough to withstand the temptation of the alcohol, and I lacked the strength to place my children's needs ahead of it. I drank more to numb the pain of the guilt.

One evening, I started a small kitchen fire when I fell asleep with food on the stove. Days later, I narrowly missed falling into the large, fully ablaze fireplace while trying to add wood. Another evening, while cooking and drinking, I had my worst accident. I took a large dish from the oven with a thin towel. When I finally felt the burn, I dropped everything. The impact sent shards of glass and hot liquid flying in every direction. No one was seriously hurt, but I was burned on both hands.

Suzi and I had only been dating for three months. She stood in the kitchen with me, bits of glass and hot liquid covering virtually every surface and asked, "What if one of the kids had been nearby?" She bandaged my burnt hands and helped me clean the mess. We were falling in love, and it was time to make a serious choice about the direction of our relationship.

"I have a young son, so if I'm going to stay in this relationship, I have to know it's safe for him and healthy for me." The next day, she asked me to give her two weeks of sobriety for her birthday. "It's all I want, Kip. But don't do it for me. You have to do it because it's what you want for yourself."

That night, with Suzi away at a teachers' conference, I thought about what she said as I poured a tall glass of vodka. I thought about a lot of things. I was worried about how much time had passed since Judge Bartle had been asked to sign the order, which would effectively finalize most of fen-phen. At one point I had wondered when he would sign, but as more time passed, I began to worry if he would sign. What could possibly be causing the delay now?

I poured a second drink.

It wasn't so much a question of whether Judge Bartle was going to approve a payment to class members and their attorneys. Most people assumed he wanted to see this massive class action become a thing of the past as much as anyone else. The concern was whether he would sign the order as it was submitted to him or whether he would tinker with it in some way.

I poured a third drink.

He certainly had the authority to make changes if he wanted, and one fear was that he would make some revision concerning attorneys' fees. As the guy with the most cases, I was also seriously invested. If he wanted, the judge could tweak fees so that I lost money, making it impossible for me to repay my massive debt.

I poured another drink. *Was it my fourth, fifth or sixth?*

Fen-phen had consumed my life. I had lived it a full ten years: through Mary Perez, Leslie's death, Debbie Lovett's trial, the media attention, the wealth, the hundred thousand clients and echocardiograms, the accusations, the RICO, a second divorce. *If I'm not careful*, I thought to myself, as I threw back the last of my drink, *it'll take me, too.*

I took the bottle of Grey Goose Vodka from the freezer and set it on the counter next to my empty glass. I was alone. My children were at their mother's, and my girlfriend was in Houston. The kitchen was large and empty. The burn spot on the floor caught my eyes. I had stomped out a burning dishtowel there the week before, lucky that I caught it before the house burned to the ground with me in it.

I looked beyond the kitchen. I had bought the house after Round One. It was large, elaborate, excessive (my kids liked to tease), and empty. The best money could buy, but empty. And if I lost money on fen-phen, I would have to sell it.

What would I have after fen-phen?

I picked up the cold bottle, turned my back to the empty glass, and put both elbows on the edge of the kitchen sink. I poured the vodka, watching and listening as it gurgled down the black hole. *Give me strength*, I prayed.

That night, prayer, not a blackout, helped me to sleep.

The following day, January 24, 2007, a copy of the judge's signed order circulated on the Internet. My email to the referring attorneys was simple and direct: "Attached is a copy of PTO 6875, which Judge Bartle signed yesterday."

I had decided the night before to try—just try—to quit drinking, and I attended two Alcoholics Anonymous meetings the morning after. It may have been a coincidence that I learned Bartle signed the order that day, but it was what I had been praying for.

That night I lay in bed painfully aware of how sober I was. It did not feel good—not yet. It was uncomfortable, painful, sickening, stressful, lonely, and the hardest thing I could remember ever doing, but I was convinced my life depended on it. Despite the discomfort, it was a rare treat for my head to hit the pillow and for me to actually be conscious of it. For a fleeting second, I thought about having a drink, but there was no vodka in the house. I had poured every drop—even my secret stashes—down the drain. Then I managed to stay busy playing pool until after the liquor stores closed. I smiled at how cleverly I had tricked the drunk inside me.

When I was at the very bottom, I had promised I would be a better person if I made it out. Now I was out. It was time to start thinking about how to make good on my promise.

That was the thought that carried me off to sleep at the end of my first sober twenty-four-hour period in many years. It was tough, but it was followed by successively easier days. They compounded, first slowly and painstakingly, and then quickly and more comfortably. After years of passing out early, I witnessed the sights and sounds of the world after dark, and they were in focus. I was sober and had no desire to ever return to drinking.

TWENTY

—❘🏛❘—

ENOUGH IS ENOUGH

WE WERE DOWN to a handful of unresolved cases by the fall of 2007. For my firm, this amounted to about sixty claims that had not received their Seventh Amendment audit for some reason. But various other firms across the country also had similar cases in the same situation, each requiring time-consuming individual attention. The final slices of the Seventh Amendment pie were being divvied, and someone had to fight for these stragglers or they would be overlooked completely.

Now I was fighting not only Fishbein, but also his newfound henchmen: Wayne and Jerry. The three of us had been a team at one point. Not two years before, we had all publicly admitted that getting this far with the Seventh Amendment would have been impossible without one another's efforts.

I had taken Jerry under my wing in Lovett and taught him everything I knew. He met people and ascended to positions he would never have reached had it not been for my influence and guidance. Other than our original agreement to work on fifteen of his cases together, which had been satisfied years earlier, we had never had financial obligations to each other. Jerry had been a friend. Wayne, on the other hand, had been a business partner. He promised to watch my back and had accepted payment for the job. When he turned on me, it was unprofessional and a betrayal to our clients.

As the Seventh Amendment payment process was about to start, Fish, by way of Wayne, began pressuring me to sign a stipulation that would initiate payments to thousands of claimants nationwide but which would, at the same time, significantly limit the rights of current and previous clients. It was broadly worded and unreasonable of him to expect me to agree, but the more I refused, the more aggressive he became. To him, the clients in question were just a few insignificant files. To me, they were some of my most important clients.

Then Jerry joined in the demands. "Kip," he wrote in an email, "you are going to have to find a way to interpret this so you can sign it."

While Wayne and Jerry hinted that my stubbornness was stalling progress on the Seventh Amendment, Fishbein did not beat around the bush. Wayne sent an email from Fish saying he would not "send the letter starting the 7th process" until I signed an agreement with respect to these stragglers.

I was disappointed to think that Wayne would give up on any of our clients or, even worse, think he could bully me into doing so. But he was now working for Fishbein, and money seemed to be his only objective. If Fish and I ever stopped fighting, Wayne and Jerry, and numerous others in Fish's employ, would receive a disproportionate cut of the half-billion in fees they were trying to get me to publicly endorse. But until they stipulated in writing to an agreed course of action on each remaining claim, I refused. This had been how the Trust had treated my clients' claims, so I had no problem being the obstacle between them and their payment.

My stubbornness led to an agreement that gave my last few clients a clear, guaranteed path to at least having their claims considered.

Fish promised to file a motion before Christmas asking Judge Bartle to order final payment to all the claimants with resolved claims. In November 2007, I traveled to Philadelphia for a hearing on the fee matter to make sure Fishbein fulfilled his part of our deal.

Wyeth's insistence on micromanaging the spending of the original $4.8 billion led to a deal in which the drug company deposited two hundred million dollars into a Fees and Costs account. It was one of the accounts from which Class Counsel would eventually be paid. Some believe this was done to buy the powerful group's assistance, a theory their unprecedented cooperation seemed to support. Wyeth, its executives, and its legal team steadfastly agreed they would never voluntarily testify in court about the peculiar funds, their creation, or their purpose. They knew, and Judge Bartle was also keenly aware, that the balance of the fund would eventually revert back to Wyeth if it did not go to the lawyers. Judge Bartle emphasized the complex nature of the matter to the sparsely attended court as he read the full title of the Omnibus Fee Motion.

"Good morning. Before the Court this morning is the Joint Petition for Final Award of Attorney's Fees and Expense Reimbursement and Partial Refund From Certain Fee Accounts in MDL-1203 and Civil Action Number 99-20593." The judge glanced about the room, as though he was taking mental attendance. "Mr. Fishbein, you may proceed."

Fishbein reminded the judge how he had requested fees before but had been denied and told to finish the job. He had done that, he explained. The settlement had "achieved its purpose." Then he said what I had come to hear: by Christmas, he would file papers asking the court to pay thousands of frustrated clients whose claims had been settled. He characterized the diet drug settlement as unprecedented in the benefits it offered, benefits that were "record-setting" in their "scale and scope." He argued that the original deal combined with the Supplemental Settlement Fund, consisting of close to seven and a half billion dollars, was the "largest class action settlement in history," a "Super-Mega-Fund" class action settlement.

After lunch, the objectors had the floor. One lawyer objected to the Class Counsel's exorbitant fee demand and their guaranteed two hundred million dollar fund from the fee and cost account. Judge Bartle replied, "Of course if the two hundred million is not paid to Class Counsel, it goes back to Wyeth. You are advocating that part of that go back to Wyeth?"

Class Counsel watched smugly with folded arms as the two hundred million dollar part of its legal bill received judicial protection. Wyeth would probably never have to explain why, almost a decade earlier, it deposited a two hundred million dollar chunk of mystery money that would be guarded and dispersed under such an air of suspicion.

Fishbein had suggested the court should consider "whose efforts produced the settlement benefits" and the "risk of non-compensation," and lawyers for the objectors wasted no time doing just that. Judge Bartle had been focusing on those same factors as they existed at the time of the settlement just weeks after our Lovett verdict back in the fall of 1999.

Brian Ripien, one of the lawyers for the objectors, argued that the MDL Plaintiffs' Management Committee and Class Counsel had very little to do with the settlement. He mentioned "Kip Petroff's verdict" and bragged about the "Texas depositions" everyone was using for trial preparation at the time. He said that it was because of these things that there was tremendous pressure on Wyeth, creating a need for a settlement in the fall of 1999. The settlement was just looking for someone to make it happen, he argued, and Class Counsel did that— but they did not do the early footwork or trench fighting to get there.

The two objectors took less than forty-five minutes to present all of their arguments. Judge Bartle then asked if there would be any rebuttal. I suspected not, and Judge Bartle's failure to pause for an answer seemed to even suggest none was needed. "Mr. Fishbein, do you wish to respond?"

One of the marks of a good trial lawyer is the ability to determine when "better is the enemy of good enough." I looked at Class Counsel's table to see if anyone there would react to any of the objector's arguments.

Fishbein rose from his seat and filled his water glass from the pitcher in front of him. He then said that he had provided a letter that my team had used in Lovett. He claimed that the letter "made the difference between a winning trial and a losing trial." He had made similar arguments shortly after the Lovett verdict, which had been untrue and which had gotten under my skin at first. But by November 2007, ten months sober and finally seeing the light at the end of the fen-phen tunnel, it was unimportant—as long as the clients got paid. I had gone through a lot in the eight years since the verdict. Recognition seemed irrelevant.

Fishbein and Class Counsel saw it differently. They needed to take credit for Lovett because it was the only verdict in existence when Wyeth agreed to pay $4.8 billion—the time period the judge was considering. Question number four on Class Counsel's slide show was "Whose Efforts Produced Settlement Benefits?" They had to claim the success was theirs in order to justify a big portion of their half billion dollar legal bill.

At Lovett, neither side relied on Fishbein's letter in closing arguments. Wyeth ridiculed it; Robert and I completely ignored it. If a piece of evidence did not warrant mention in closing arguments, it had not been that special.

In many ways, Fishbein had just given me exactly what I had wanted for years: a way to humiliate him as he had me on numerous occasions. It was too easy. He was handing me the weapon and constructing the platform to launch it. I had every right to stand and challenge his claims. How could a lawyer with a half billion dollar legal bill leave himself so vulnerable?

Even though I was not scheduled to speak at the hearing, Judge Bartle would probably let me respond. After all, it was my verdict in question and both sides had mentioned it in their arguments. It would probably feel good to humiliate Fish and all the other class action fat cats who were licking their greedy lips, waiting to feed on the half billion in fees.

I stood and walked to the aisle, placed my belongings on the bench and buttoned my coat, never taking my eyes off Fish. He shifted his weight and seemed to sense my movement behind him, glancing slightly over his shoulder. His profile, his methods and the notion he would soon be swimming in dirty money turned my stomach.

Judge Bartle glanced from the papers in front of him to the men and women scattered around the nearly empty courtroom, passing over me without hesitation, and then back to the stack of papers. I did the same. There were a few familiar, supportive faces. We exchanged friendly half-smiles, and then I gathered my things and walked slowly down the aisle.

It had been a long journey. I was no longer the man I used to be. When this battle against Goliath first started, it had just been me and about fifty clients—even though five times that many had asked me to represent them. But I had been selective, meeting with each client, fighting for each person's cause. It had been a good fight, but the war had changed. With time, quantity won out over quality, and I lost sight of the fact that each person was my most important concern. I became a celebrity. Everyone was my friend, but I could trust almost no one, and there was a price on my head. I hated who I had become, and I wanted to get back to something meaningful.

I knew what had to be done. Each step felt like it was taking me in the wrong direction, but in my heart, I knew it was right. The journey needed to come to an end, and this was the only way I could do it. *It's time,* I thought.

The long, brass handle was cold in my grip. *If I keep going,* I thought, *there's no turning back.* The handle clicked. Maybe it was my imagination, but it seemed louder than it should have been, as were the whispers and sounds of shifting bodies. I pushed the door open, took in a deep breath, and left Judge Bartle's courtroom behind me.

The bright light from the windows ahead was a sharp contrast to the dimly lit courtroom. My eyes shut while they adapted just as the door clicked behind me. *It's over,* I thought, *finally done.* The next few seconds seemed like an eternity. The weight, the burden, the lies, the sleaziness, the accusations, the past—it was all behind me.

In front of me was a life without constant daily threats.

The elevator was empty; I took it down to the lobby alone. There was still a lot of work to do. Plus, I had decided to take up a new hobby, something that would be impossible if I was still drinking. I would start writing a book—the story of my fen-phen journey.

They say the pen is mightier than the sword. It is time to stop fighting my old adversaries. Instead, I will write about them.

AFTERWORD

FORBES CALLED IT the "22 Billion Dollar Gold Rush" in March 2006. With nothing even remotely similar for a historical comparison, early fen-phen forecasters had no inkling of the scope of the drugs' economic impact. The pills, together with the seemingly endless litigation that followed their demise, have caused greater financial damage and personal injury than anyone could have imagined.

In March 1999, when the first case was starting trial, *The Dallas Morning News* article "Fen-phen suit in Texas seen as 'road test,'" reported that Wall Street analysts thought AHP would be able to weather potential losses due to a one billion dollar insurance policy. It was suggested that court defeats would result in little more than a few worried investors and some possible headlines, but the author doubted that the trouble would have any material effect on the company.

That could not have been further from the truth. In the end, the result was a class action settlement of more than seven billion dollars involving over six million class members, hundreds of law firms, countless legal briefs, dozens of jury verdicts ranging from zero to a billion dollars, and billions more in opt-out payments.

In April 2008, eleven years after fen-phen users last took the drugs, Judge Bartle finally issued his Final Memorandum and Order. He explained in detail his reasoning for approving the half billion dollar payment to Class Counsel. One justification was the fee application that Wayne negotiated behind my back and then convinced me to sign. In short, the judge suggested that attorneys with the greatest numbers of cases used the MDL's work to bolster their own, and if they supported the MDL's fee, then the MDL deserved to receive it. The half billion dollar legal bill was going to be paid. So were the claimants. The drug company that had threatened to ruin me had instead been made to pay again, and they were willing to walk away from it all. It was time to let go.

More than five million people never received the free echocardiograms that were supposedly available through the Trust in 2002; most of them forever lost their right to make a claim by the screening deadline in January 2003.

Despite all the threats and accusations, no one ever again tried to disqualify any of the hotel echocardiograms. All but a very few of our nearly one hundred thousand echos met the basic criteria necessary to assert a claim.

Ironically, clients found eligible for full payment under the Seventh Amendment received about the same amount of money as they would have received in the original deal.

American Home Products changed its name to Wyeth in 2002 and then sold out completely to Pfizer, another drug powerhouse, in 2009. The company, under whatever name, spent roughly twenty-two billion dollars cleaning up after fen-phen. In the fall of 2011, at this book's printing, there was well over a billion dollars remaining unclaimed in the Settlement Trust. Almost all the Seventh Amendment claims are resolved, and the Trust, today, is engaged almost exclusively in processing surgery and death claims. The $1.275 billion added under the Seventh Amendment provided financial security for the benefit of claimants. Yet, we still fight the Trust for payment on what are clearly legitimate claims.

My version of this case is only one man's perspective. Numerous documents, stories, lies and truths have yet to be revealed. Because it is a case polluted with secrecy, we will probably never know the full scope: the depths to which some sank, the breadth of lies, secret pacts, and intimidation. Nor will we uncover the high ranks contaminated with greed or malice. For every secret our investigation has revealed, there are many more we will probably never know.

In the beginning, Robert and I knew each client by name, and while I may have lost that in the past, it is how we again strive to operate today. We still fight for each and every one of our clients, and each claim is a battle for fair compensation. But at least the war is over.

Wayne's civil RICO threat against me never materialized; I never even received a target letter from the Trust or the U.S. Attorneys' office. Years later, Wayne Spivey would testify that he could not remember warning me that a ruinous RICO suit was right around the corner, probably because it never was. But without the RICO threat, Wayne could never have demanded a doubling of his fee a few weeks later.

In both court and arbitration years later, and after five days of contentious testimony from Wayne, Jerry, Mike Fishbein, me, and others, the arbitration panel unanimously took my side. But Wayne refused to accept the panel's decision and appealed. As of the printing of this book in 2011, we continue to duke it out in the Dallas Court of Civil Appeals.

So a dozen years after the drugs' removal from the market, those who never even took fenfluramine or phentermine fill their deep pockets while millions of trusting former fen-phen users wonder if this is the day their heart disease will make itself known—and if not, they wonder how long their luck will hold.

The fen-phen clock continues ticking.

ABOUT THE AUTHORS

KIP A. PETROFF has been suing large companies on behalf of injured consumers for more than twenty-five years, but is best known for blazing the trail in the fen-phen diet drug litigation. He is the founder and senior partner of the Dallas-based firm, Petroff & Associates, and is board certified by the Texas Board of Legal Specialization in both civil and personal injury trial law.

He lives in Dallas, Texas with his wife, Suzi, and their blended family. Together they founded New Hope Foundation, a nonprofit organization dedicated to improving the living conditions of underprivileged families. One hundred percent of the profits from the sale of *Battling Goliath: Inside a $22 Billion Legal Scandal*, will benefit New Hope Foundation.

Petroff has been featured in *The Wall Street Journal, The New York Times, USA TODAY, Time* magazine, *U.S. News & World Report*, and *Lawyers Weekly USA* and has appeared on *Good Morning America, Sixty Minutes II, CNN, Burden of Proof, Frontline, Fox News*, and *NBC Nightly News*.

Petroff welcomes visitors and messages at his website: www.petroffassociates.com.

SUZI ZIMMERMAN PETROFF is a former teacher and author of numerous books and theatrical pieces. She uses her teaching and parenting experience to volunteer with and advise young people, which is the topic of her forthcoming book. She has two sons, three stepchildren, and is married to Kip Petroff. Learn more about Zimmerman Petroff at www.meriwhetherpublishing.com and www.suzizimmerman.com.

GLOSSARY

The following definitions are intended to assist the reader in understanding certain terms as. These are abbreviated definitions intended solely to assist the reader in understanding certain terms , and they may not be entirely accurate for any other purpose.

A.H. ROBINS The original company that developed and sold Pondimin. American Home Products later purchased A.H. Robins in 1989.

AHP SETTLEMENT TRUST (THE TRUST) The entity charged with administering the Nationwide Settlement.

ALLI A weight loss drug approved by the Food and Drug Administration (FDA) for over the counter sale.

ALTERNATIVE CLAIMS FACILITY This is where the money is for the Seventh Amendment.

AMENDMENT A change to a class action settlement is sometimes called an amendment.

AMERICAN HOME PRODUCTS (AHP) This is the parent company of Wyeth Ayerst, the maker of Pondimin and Redux. American Home Products is sometimes referred to as AHP or Wyeth.

ARNOLD & PORTER Arnold & Porter is one of the law firms that represented Wyeth.

BLACK BOX A warning on a drug's package insert that is surrounded by a solid black line to highlight it.

CIVIL RICO COMPLAINT A legal document filed with a court alleging that someone violated the Racketeer Influenced & Corrupt Organization Act, 18 U.S.C. §§ 1961-1968.

CLAIMS ADMINISTRATION The process of analyzing and approving or rejecting a claim for compensation. The supervision of echocardiograms is mentioned in the "Claims Administration" section of the Nationwide Settlement Agreement.

CLASS ACTION A type of lawsuit where numerous people's claims are joined together into one lawsuit.

CLASS COUNSEL The lawyers appointed by the federal judge to act as "counsel" for the "class." They agreed to serve as lawyers for all the class members, including class members with lawyers as well as those without lawyers. The terms "Class Counsel" and "Plaintiffs' Management Committee" or "MDL Plaintiffs' Management Committee" are sometimes used interchangeably.

CLASS MEMBER People who ingested Pondimin or Redux were considered part of the class action Nationwide Settlement and were sometimes referred to as "class members."

CO-COUNSEL A lawyer who is working on a case together with another lawyer or group of lawyers.

COMPLAINT A legal document filed with a court alleging that someone is liable for damages due to some improper conduct. "Petition" is synonymous with complaint.

COURT OF APPEALS A court where a case is taken if a party to a lawsuit wants to try to overturn or "reverse" a trial judge's decision.

DEFENDANT The party that is sued when a lawsuit is filed.

GLOSSARY

DEPOSITION Sworn testimony that is typically given outside of court but can usually be used in court.

DISCOVERY REQUESTS Written documents served on a party to a lawsuit pursuant to applicable rules of procedure. Typical discovery requests in civil litigation include requests for depositions, interrogatories, requests for admissions, document production requests, and requests for inspection.

ECHOMOTION A company in Chapel Hill, North Carolina that performed echocardiograms for Petroff & Associates and other law firms in Round Two.

ECHOCARDIOGRAM (ECHO) This is the gold standard test for determining if a person has heart valve leakage. It involves the same technology as the sonogram done on a pregnant woman; it just involves the heart rather than the pelvic area.

ECHOMOTION MOTION A legal motion filed with the MDL seeking to have all echocardiograms conducted by EchoMotion disqualified due to lack of supervision.

FDA APPROVAL The Food and Drug Administration determined that a drug company should be allowed to market and sell the drug in the United States.

FDA POSITIVE The Food and Drug Administration coined this term in 1997 to refer to a patient's heart valve condition. A person is "FDA Positive" if they have at least mild aortic valve leakage or at least moderate mitral valve leakage.

FEN-PHEN The combination of two diet drugs. The "fen" is derived from fenfluramine or dexfenfluramine. The "phen" is derived from phentermine, a speed-like drug that, as of 2011, is still on the market. This name is sometimes used generically to refer to any combination of drugs using Pondimin (fenfluramine) or Redux (dexfenfluramine) with or without phentermine.

FINAL JUDICIAL APPROVAL The term "Final Judicial Approval" is a defined term in the Settlement Agreement that triggers certain deadlines and obligations under the Settlement Agreement. It means Judge Bechtle's approval of the original Settlement Agreement and Judge Bartle's approval of the Seventh Amendment had become final by the exhaustion of all appeals.

GENERAL CAUSATION The ability of a drug to cause a certain illness in some people.

GREEN FORM This is the claim form used to seek Matrix Level Benefits. For an example of the "Matrix" portion of the green form, see page 191.

HOTEL ECHO A "hotel echo" is the term given to an echocardiogram performed in a hotel.

INTERNEURON The company that originally held the Redux patent.

JUDGMENT A judgment is a written decision by a court or other tribunal that resolves a controversy and determines the rights and obligations of the parties.

JUDICIAL PANEL ON MULTI-DISTRICT LITIGATION (JPMDL) A JPMDL is a group or "panel" of federal judges who make decisions concerning whether case management and discovery issues in certain groups of federal cases should be considered together in front of one judge.

JURY CHARGE The questions that a jury in Texas is asked to answer when deciding a civil case.

MASS TORT "Mass tort" usually refers to a large group of cases where the plaintiffs in almost all the cases are making similar allegations against a common defendant or group of defendants. Fen-phen litigation was a mass tort involving tens of thousands of plaintiffs asserting similar claims against the same group of defendants.

MASTER FEE AGREEMENT The document many plaintiff's lawyers signed in support of the Joint Fee Application filed with the court requesting more than half a billion dollars in legal fees.

MATRIX The Matrix is the chart that shows how much money a claimant will receive if his or her claim is approved based on the individual's age at diagnosis, duration of drug usage, and medical condition as documented by echo before the end of the screening period. For more information, see the "Matrix" portion of the green form, page 191.

MDL PLAINTIFFS' MANAGEMENT COMMITTEE (PMC) The PMC is a committee of lawyers established by Judge Bechtle to oversee and coordinate the consolidated pretrial proceedings and to conduct discovery on behalf of the plaintiffs. The terms "Class Counsel" and "Plaintiffs' Management Committee" or "MDL Plaintiffs' Management Committee" are sometimes used interchangeably.

MEDICAL MONITOR A medical monitor was a Wyeth employee who was in charge of receiving and analyzing adverse event reports related to certain drugs.

MEDICAL MONITORING SUIT A medical monitoring lawsuit was any lawsuit that sought to obtain free echos for certain fen-phen users.

MITRAL REGURGITATION Mitral regurgitation is a condition that occurs when the normal flow of blood in the heart is interrupted and some blood flows backward across the mitral heart valve. Valve "regurgitation" or "insufficiency" are synonymous with "leakage."

MITRAL VALVE A normal person has four heart valves. The two on the left side (aortic and mitral) are the two associated with fen-phen toxicity.

MOTION A motion is a legal document filed with a court asking the court to take specific action in a case.

MULTI-DISTRICT LITIGATION (MDL) An MDL is a procedural device frequently used to consolidate class or individual actions brought in federal court for pre-trial purposes. The MDL statute is 28 U.S.C. § 1407.

OPT OUT This term is used as a verb and a noun. A person is an "opt-out" if they chose to reject or "opt out" of the Nationwide Settlement and file a lawsuit instead.

ORDER An order is a legal decision from a court.

PETITION A petition is the document that a person or organization files with a court when the individual or organization sues another person or organization. ("Complaint" is synonymous with petition.)

PETITION TO INTERVENE The Petition to Intervene was a pleading Petroff & Associates filed asking Judge Bechtle to let the firm contend that its work created a "common benefit" that resulted in the Nationwide Settlement Agreement.

PHARMACOTHERAPY The term pharmacotherapy refers to a prescriptive drug protocol as the treatment of a medical condition.

PHENTERMINE Phentermine is a generic amphetamine-like drug used in the fen-phen combination. The "phen" in fen-phen is derived from phentermine.

PLAINTIFF The plaintiff is the person or organization that files a lawsuit.

PONDIMIN Pondimin is the "fen" in fen-phen. It is also known as

GLOSSARY

fenfluramine.

PPH This is the acronym for primary pulmonary hypertension, a disease that is caused by fen-phen.

PROXIMATE CAUSE A jury in a Texas civil case is asked if a defendant's conduct or product was a proximate cause of injury; it is legally sufficient to result in liability if it was a proximate cause of injury.

PUNITIVE DAMAGES Punitive damages are damages awarded in addition to actual damages when the defendant acted with recklessness, malice, or deceit.

REDUX Redux is the new and improved Pondimin. It is virtually identical chemically and pharmacologically to Pondimin.

REQUEST FOR PRODUCTION OF DOCUMENTS In pretrial discovery, a party's written request that another party provide specified documents or other tangible things for inspection and copying is referred to as a Request for Production of Documents.

REVERSE BIFURCATION Reverse bifurcation is the process of splitting or dividing a trial into two phases whereby the jury first determines the extent of a person's drug-related injuries in phase one and then determines whether the company is liable for those injuries in phase two.

ROUND ONE Round One refers to the period of time from the day the drugs were removed from the market in 1997 until sometime around May 2003 when the second opt-out period began.

ROUND TWO Round Two refers to the period of time from around May 2003 until all the opt-out cases were resolved.

SCREENING PERIOD The screening period is the twelve-month period following the Final Judicial Approval of the Settlement Agreement during which time free echocardiograms were supposed to be available in the screening program (January 3, 2002 to January 3, 2003). In the Fifth Amendment, the screening period was extended six months for certain eligible Class Members.

SCREENING PROGRAM The screening program generally refers to the AHP Settlement Trust's program for providing free echocardiograms to diet drug users during the screening period.

SEVENTH AMENDMENT The Seventh Amendment is the seventh and largest change or "amendment" to the Nationwide Settlement. This change involved creating a whole new "settlement within a settlement." It involved Wyeth putting more than a billion dollars of new money into a new, amended Nationwide Settlement.

SEVENTH AMENDMENT LIAISON COMMITTEE (SALC) The SALC was a committee of lawyers appointed by Judge Bartle to assist in the implementation of the Seventh Amendment as liaison between counsel for Class Members, on the one hand, and Class Counsel, Wyeth and the court, on the other hand.

SONOGRAPHER A sonographer is a person licensed to perform an echocardiogram. "Echo tech" and sonographer are used interchangeably.

SOURCE OF ECHO FORM The source of echo form is a document that the Trust's special counsel sent to some lawyers asking about the echocardiogram being used to support a claim that the lawyer filed with the trust.

SPECIFIC CAUSATION A drug is a "specific cause" of a disease or illness if it creates that illness in that person.

STATUTE OF LIMITATIONS The statute of limitations is the time period in which a person must bring a lawsuit or they will be "barred by the statute of limitations."

SUBPOENA When used as a noun, a subpoena is a writ demanding a person to appear before a court or other tribunal, subject to a penalty for failing to comply. When used as a verb, the term refers to the calling of a person or organization before a court or other tribunal by subpoena.

SUPERVISION Supervision is an undefined term used in the Claims Administration section of the Nationwide Settlement Agreement. A major point of contention in Round Two was whether certain echocardiograms were properly supervised.

SUPPLEMENTAL SETTLEMENT FUND The "Supplemental Settlement Fund" is the money that was in the Seventh Amendment.

TARRANT COUNTY DOCUMENT DEPOSITORY The Tarrant County Document Depository is the building where all the defendants in Tarrant County deposited documents and other information that was produced in response to discovery requests served in the Tarrant County fen-phen cases.

TARRANT COUNTY STEERING COMMITTEE This was a group of lawyers who helped coordinate management of fen-phen cases in Tarrant County, Texas.

TOLLING AGREEMENTS Tolling agreements refers to documents that would extend or "toll" the statute of limitations against whoever signed it. These agreements are used so that a person with a right to file a lawsuit does not have to worry about filing it by the statute of limitations date because that date is extended by virtue of the signed agreement.

TRANSCRIPTS "Transcripts" are written, word-for-word records of what was said, either in a proceeding such as a trial or during some other conversation, as in a transcript of a hearing or oral deposition.

VALVE A normal person has four heart valves. The two on the left side (aortic and mitral) are the two associated with fen-phen toxicity.

VALVE LEAKAGE Valve leakage is a condition that occurs when the normal flow of blood in the heart is interrupted and some blood flows backward across the heart valve. Valve "regurgitation" or "insufficiency" are synonymous with "leakage."

VALVE SURGERY Valve surgery is an operation on a heart valve.

VINSON & ELKINS This is one of the law firms that represented Wyeth in Round One and Round Two.

WRITTEN INTERROGATORIES Written interrogatories are written question(s) submitted to an opposing party in a lawsuit as part of discovery.

WYETH Wyeth Ayerst Laboratories Division was the division of American Home Products that sold Pondimin and Redux.

iet Drug Settlement With
american Home Products Corporation

ettlement Matrix Compensation Benefits Guide
r Physicians, Attorneys and Class Members

A Nationwide Class Action Settlement has been reached with American Home Products Corporation, which will resolve the claims of individuals who took the diet drugs Pondimin® and/or Redux™.

Under the Settlement, patients who took the diet drugs Pondimin® and/or Redux™ have a right to receive compensation if they have developed serious levels of valvular heart disease.

The amounts which individuals are entitled to recover under this Settlement depend on the person's age at diagnosis of valvular heart disease, the person's "Level of Severity" and additional criteria as set forth below. Payments will be made according to these "Matrices":

trix A-1 — Age at diagnosis/event

erity	≤24	25-29	30-34	35-39	40-44	45-49	50-54	55-59	60-64	65-69	70-79
	$123,750	$117,563	$111,685	$106,100	$100,795	$95,755	$90,967	$86,419	$82,098	$73,888	$36,944
	$643,500	$611,325	$580,759	$551,721	$524,135	$497,928	$473,032	$449,381	$426,912	$384,221	$192,111
	$940,500	$893,475	$848,801	$806,361	$766,043	$727,741	$691,354	$656,786	$623,947	$561,552	$280,776
	$1,336,500	$1,269,675	$1,206,191	$1,145,881	$1,088,587	$1,034,158	$982,450	$933,327	$886,661	$797,995	$398,998
	$1,485,000	$1,410,750	$1,340,213	$1,273,202	$1,209,542	$1,149,065	$1,091,612	$1,037,031	$985,180	$886,662	$443,331

trix B-1 — Age at diagnosis/event

erity	≤24	25-29	30-34	35-39	40-44	45-49	50-54	55-59	60-64	65-69	70-79
	$24,750	$23,513	$22,337	$21,221	$20,159	$19,152	$18,194	$17,284	$16,420	$14,778	$7,389
	$128,700	$122,265	$116,152	$110,344	$104,827	$99,586	$94,606	$89,876	$85,383	$76,844	$38,422
	$188,100	$178,695	$169,760	$161,272	$153,208	$145,548	$138,270	$131,357	$124,790	$112,310	$56,155
	$267,300	$253,935	$241,238	$229,176	$217,717	$206,831	$196,489	$186,665	$177,332	$159,599	$79,800
	$297,000	$282,150	$268,043	$254,641	$241,908	$229,813	$218,322	$207,406	$197,036	$177,332	$88,666

The circumstances which determine whether "Matrix A-1" or "Matrix B-1" is applicable are as follows:

1. **For Matrix A-1:** Diet Drug Recipients who ingested Pondimin® and/or Redux™ for 61 or more days, who were diagnosed as FDA Positive, whose conditions are eligible for matrix payments but who do not have any condition or circumstance which makes Matrix B-1 applicable, receive payments on Matrix A-1.

2. **For Matrix B-1:** Diet Drug Recipients who are eligible for matrix payments and to whom one or more of the following conditions apply, receive payments on Matrix B-1:

    • For claims as to the mitral valve, Diet Drug Recipients who were diagnosed as having Mild Mitral Regurgitation (regardless of the duration of ingestion of Pondimin® and/or Redux™).

GREEN FORM - 16

INDEX

INDEX

INDEX